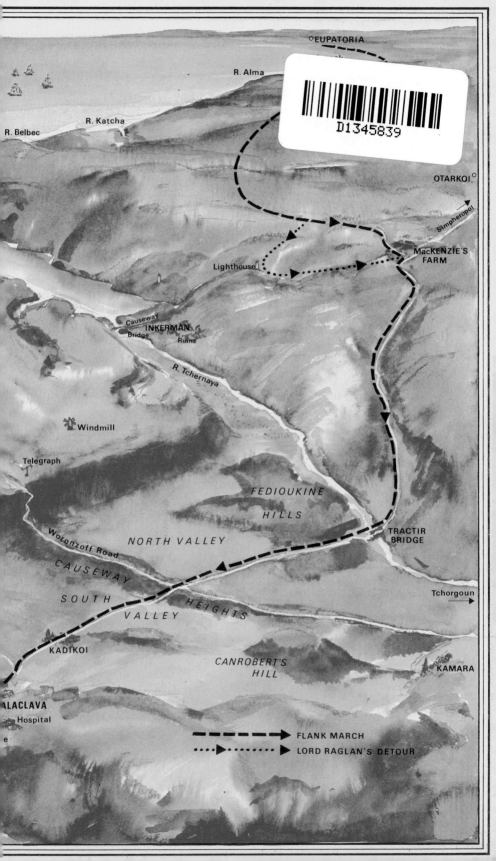

EUPATORIA

R. Alma

R. Katcha

R. Belbec

OTARKOI

Simpheropol

Lighthouse

MacKENZIE'S FARM

Causeway
Bridge   INKERMAN
          Ruins

R. Tchernaya

Windmill

Telegraph

FEDIOUKINE
HILLS

TRACTIR
BRIDGE

Wotonzoff Road

NORTH VALLEY

CAUSEWAY

Tchorgoun

SOUTH   HEIGHTS
VALLEY

KADIKOI

CANROBERT'S
HILL

KAMARA

ALACLAVA

Hospital
e

FLANK MARCH

LORD RAGLAN'S DETOUR

THE THIN RED LINE

*The story of the Battle of Balaclava
told by some of those who were there*

The Thin Red Line

THE THIN RED LINE
of Balaclava

JOHN SELBY

HAMISH HAMILTON
LONDON

First published in Great Britain 1970
by Hamish Hamilton Ltd
90 Great Russell Street London WC1

Copyright © 1970 by John Selby

SBN 241 01900 1

Printed in Great Britain
by Westerham Press Ltd Westerham Kent

CONTENTS

Foreword by Major-General F. C. Graham, C.B., D.S.O.,
Colonel Argyll and Sutherland Highlanders

PART I

PART II

PART III

BIBLIOGRAPHY

APPENDIX A

The Victoria Cross and the Cross of St. George

APPENDIX B

Present designation of regiments mentioned in this book

LIST OF ILLUSTRATIONS

INDEX

ACKNOWLEDGEMENTS

I wish to thank my colleague at the R.M.A. Sandhurst, Mr. Antony Brett-James, for giving me the opportunity of writing this book and providing several valuable sources; Mr. Richard Holmes for information on the Cross of St. George; Mr. King of the Ministry of Defence (Central and Army) Library for yet again putting the benefit of his wide knowledge at my disposal; Major R. G. Bartelot of the Royal Artillery Institution, Woolwich, for help on artillery matters; and Officer Cadet I. H. McNeil of my Military History Set at Sandhurst for compiling the appendices. I also wish to thank my publisher, Mr. Christopher Sinclair-Stevenson of Hamish Hamilton Ltd, for his courteous help and advice.

FOREWORD

The Crimean War has exercised a strange fascination among historians, poets, artists and novelists.

How was this fascination inspired? The cause for which the British and their Allies fought was not particularly honourable or glamorous. The basic *casus belli* could be simply the desire to teach a salutary lesson to the Tsar and his looming legions. The majority of British people had never heard of the Crimea.

As so often before, and it was to happen again, the fascination lay in the magnificent courage and hardihood of the young leaders and rank and file of the Army. Although Parliament and the public might fulminate against the habits of the soldiery in times of peace, regarding them as drunken rogues and neglecting their administration and welfare, in war it was different. Now the soldier became the national hero, a splendid figure in his fine uniform, representing Britain's might against the Muscovite barbarian, expected to be worthy of his hire – meagre though it was. In the Crimea the Army justified the trust placed in it beyond the bounds of belief. The military hierarchy in the Horse Guards, deprived of the master hand of the Duke of Wellington by his recent death, was incapable of implementing his doctrines. The failure to provide proper administration for the expeditionary force was nearly catastrophic. Hunger, cold, dirt, disease, lack of medical stores and amenities of any kind, caused havoc in the ranks of an Army dumped into an arid, unhealthy land and out-numbered against a powerful enemy in the company of allies of uncertain temperament. Yet over all these horrors the undaunted toughness of the rank and file triumphed. The war became the back drop for epics in its history which the Army, and it is hoped the public too, can never forget.

The Alma, the charges of the Heavy and Light Brigades, the Thin Red Line and Inkerman, the soldiers' battle, are the epics which have been commemorated in prose, verse, song, music and pictures.

The author of this book has not involved himself in a discussion of strategy and tactics – he has, with great pains, produced a factual story which portrays, in all its stark misery, the sort of life led by a soldier in the Crimea and how he died. His account of the life of the Russian garrison in Sebastopol and the miseries of the besieged is a particularly absorbing chapter in his narrative. The life of a staff officer in operations of this kind was not one of ease and safety as was often supposed by those 'at the sharp end' and the existence of Captain Ewart on joining the Commander-in-Chief's Staff was, to say the least, eventful. Some eighty-six years later the young liaison officers attached to the H.Q. of the Commander of the 8th Army performed day to day duties strangely reminiscent of the adventures of Captain Ewart.

Once again the endurance of the British soldier survived the ordeal and, in spite of the tragic blunders and callous neglect of those in high places at home, the Commanders in the field and the men they led saved the day and confounded Queen Victoria's enemies. The author records that this has been called 'the last Gentleman's War', but it was also a private soldier's war whether artilleryman, trooper, guardsman or highlander – these were men indeed.

F. C. C. Graham,
Major-General C.B., D.S.O.,
Colonel,
The Argyll & Sutherland Highlanders

INTRODUCTION

INTRODUCTION

Balaclava has been described by weaving together substantial extracts from the accounts of eye-witnesses. For the early part of the battle – the retreat from the redoubts, and the stand of the 93rd – the narrators were Lord George Paget of the 4th Light Dragoons, Lieutenant Roberts, Royal Marine Artillery, Surgeon Munro of the 93rd, Sir John Blunt who was Lord Lucan's interpreter, Lieutenant F. T. Whinyates of I Troop R.H.A., and Mrs. Duberly. For the Charge of the Heavy Brigade, the accounts of A. W. Kinglake, the historian of the War, and of Major Forrest, 4th Dragoon Guards, were used; for the Charge of the Light Brigade, those of William Russell, the *Times* correspondent, Lord George Paget, and Private Wightman of the 17th Lancers. For the last part of the battle and the arrival of the 4th Division, the narrator was Captain Ewart.

For the periods before and after the battle, other eye-witness accounts have also been followed, including those of Private George Greig of the 93rd, Captain Henry Clifford of the Rifle Brigade, Captain Hodasevich of the Russian Taroutine Regiment and Captains Adye and Hamley of the Royal Artillery (the latter the author of *Operations of War*).

Most of the sources have been used before, but there is new material from the letters of Sir John Blunt and Lieutenant Roberts, and also from the letters of *le capitaine* Henri Loizillon and *le colonel* de Wimpffen, and from the report of General Marmora commanding the Sardinian army. The information concerning cholera was taken from Surgeon Buzzard's book.

The accounts used most extensively were those of Surgeon Munro, Captain Ewart and Captain Hodasevich. These three comment in a human and interesting way on the war. The next source most used was Lord George Paget's diary. He appears to have been very observant and emerges as a most likable person. The journal of Mrs. Duberly and her *Letters to Selina* have also been used freely, particularly in the chapter covering the stay of the allied armies in Bulgaria and in the early stages of the Battle of Balaclava. Finally, for the relatively small amount of background material, the *Cambridge Modern History*, Kinglake's and Nolan's great works and William Russell's books have been used. The latter, as correspondent of *The Times* newspaper, watched the battle from the top of the cliffs along the eastern edge of the Chersonese Plateau along with A. W. Kinglake, the historian of the war.

William Russell may have been the first to use the expression 'The Thin Red Line', for in his reports he wrote of 'that thin red streak tipped with a line of steel', and in 1895, in correspondence, he claimed that he changed the original phrase into 'the thin red line tipped with steel' in his book published in 1877. There are, however, other possible claimants: for example, Sir Charles Staveley, commanding the 44th, wrote in his diary that he was in Balaclava when the firing broke out, and as he rode up to Kadikoi saw 'the thin red line of the 93rd Highlanders fire their celebrated volleys'; then, in 1873, the Lord Provost of Edinburgh is recorded as addressing the 93rd as 'The Thin Red Line of Alma and Balaclava'. The 93rd's journal was called *The Thin Red Line* until the regiment amalgamated with the Argylls; and after Balaclava the expression became appropriate for any description of British soldiers making a stand, for Kipling in his famous poem 'Tommy' speaks of 'the thin red line of 'eroes when the drums begin to roll'.

Russell whose despatches were largely instrumental in rousing public opinion in England against inefficient army administration, and in bringing about a change of ministry, had some admirers in the Crimea. Captain Henry Clifford of the Rifle Brigade, who was A.D.C. to General Buller, wrote about the splendid articles in *The Times* on the condition of the army and staff, saying that Russell's letters gave a true and not exaggerated account of the state the army was in. Russell, he said, had spoken out even more frankly after he was chased from headquarters by Lord Raglan for giving information in his letters which might be useful to the Russians. He might be thought a vulgar low Irishman, an apostate Catholic, but that was neither here nor there. He had the gift of the gab, and used his pen as well as his tongue, sang a good song, drank anyone's brandy and water, and smoked as many cigars as foolish young officers would let him. He was looked upon by most in the camp as a 'Jolly Good Fellow'. He was just the sort of chap to get information, particularly out of youngsters, and more than one nob had thought best to give him a shake of the hand rather than a cold shoulder; for *The Times'* own correspondent was rather an awkward gentleman to be on bad

2

terms with. He was not popular at Clifford's own headquarters, though. He had written about Buller's Brigade 'having been somewhat mismanaged' at Alma, and had made a bitter enemy of General Buller. But Henry Clifford did not think that Master Russell fretted much about that, and believed there was no doubt the day would come when, if his general did not forget and forgive, he would see his name spoken of even less pleasingly in 'The Paper of the World'.

Another person present at Balaclava was Mrs. Henry Duberly, the wife of Captain Duberly of the 8th Hussars. Having managed with some difficulty to reach the seat of war, she was ensconced in the *Star of the South* in Balaclava Harbour amongst the jammed transports near *Dryad*, the yacht of Lord Cardigan, the commander of the Light Brigade. Lord Cardigan had connived at her coming to the Crimea; he entertained her frequently on his yacht; and he lent her horses to ride, including his famous chestnut Ronald of the Charge. There has been speculation as to the nature of their friendship. A recent film portrayed them as lovers, and very crudely. It showed them, after a dinner on board, helping each other off with their corsets, and then his lordship laying Fanny across his knees and slapping her behind. There is really no evidence for this. On the contrary, she is recorded as making rude remarks about Lord Cardigan – like many others – and as saying she detested him; but she was often in his company, and this did not pass without comment as she herself noticed. In a letter of 11 September 1854 to her sister Selina she wrote that even with only three ladies – and on different ships – the gossip was intolerable.

These were the observers. Important also to an understanding of this book is a brief survey of the commanders, whose virtues and weaknesses were embedded in their decisions, vital to success or failure in the campaign.

The Russian commander-in-chief at Balaclava was Prince Mentschikoff. He was well served by his subordinates inside Sebastopol, for it is hard to believe that anyone could have done better in the defence of that city than Admiral Korniloff and Colonel Todleben. Indeed Todleben's defence tactics won him immortal fame. In the field, however, the prince was less well supported. He was prone to accept his subordinate commanders at their own valuation, and suffered because of it. At Balaclava, General Jabrokritsky allowed his guns to be overrun by a charge of the Chasseurs d'Afrique, and General Ryjoff's cavalry were not well directed. Only General Liprandi showed initiative; he carried through a forceful attack by stimulating his infantry with threats that their gunners behind had orders to pepper them if they faltered.

The principal British commanders at Balaclava were Lord Raglan, the Duke of Cambridge, General Scarlett, General Cathcart, Lord Lucan, Lord Cardigan and Sir Colin Campbell; but the last three were most involved.

Lord Raglan was the youngest of the Duke of Beaufort's eleven children. He was first commissioned at the age of fifteen in the 4th Light Dragoons, but later transferred to the 42nd. He had been present at Roliça, Vimiero, Talavera, and Busaco under the Duke of Wellington, and wherever he fought he showed great bravery. On Christmas Day 1810 he was made Military Secretary; but this did not preclude him from active duty, for in 1812 he climbed up the bastion of San Vicente at Badajoz and helped bring about the surrender of the fortress. He was at Waterloo in 1815, where he had his right elbow smashed by a musket-ball from a French sniper on the roof of the farmhouse of La Haye Sainte. He walked back to a cottage used as a forward hospital and suffered the amputation of his right arm with complete composure. When the arm was tossed away by the surgeon, he called out, 'Hey, bring my arm back. I want the ring my wife gave me on a finger.' He had a happy private life and was well liked, and he remained popular with the army even when much went wrong for which he could be held responsible as supreme commander. Lord Raglan watched the battle from the top of the cliffs. He did not play much part, and the little he did do was unfortunate.

The Duke of Cambridge commanded the First Division. He was the thirty-five-year-old grandson of George III, and a cousin of Queen Victoria. He had been colonel of a Hanoverian regiment at nine and a major-general at twenty-six. He was a good-natured man, industrious, well liked and affable. He played a very small part at Balaclava only arriving with his division at the very end.

Major-General the Hon. James Scarlett was elderly, but sensible, pleasant and easy-going and much liked in the army. He led the charge of the Heavy Brigade most boldly and successfully.

The Hon. Sir George Cathcart took part only in the last phase of the battle. He was commissioned in the Life Guards and after a succession of purchases acquired the command of the 7th Hussars. Touchy, inexperienced, stubborn and tactless, he did not get on well with Lord Raglan.

Finally, there were the three commanders most concerned at

Balaclava: Lord Lucan, Lord Cardigan and Sir Colin Campbell. The two senior cavalry leaders were very odd; and as their eccentricities, and quarrels, were well known, it was thought that the authorities had acted unwisely in sending them out to the Crimea in the same division.

In 1826, as George Bingham, Lord Lucan bought the command of the 17th Lancers. He poured money into the regiment and turned them out so splendidly that they became known as 'Bingham's Dandies'. He was a perfectionist, and by constantly reprimanding the officers and flogging the men, created at first-class regiment – and one always well reported on at annual inspections. But although conscientious and very hardworking, he was also narrow-minded and vindictive, and unpopular with his officers. In 1828 he saw service with the Russians in their war against the Turks in the Balkans and showed himself to be indifferent to hardship and very courageous.

His brother-in-law, Lord Cardigan, had most of his faults and few of his virtues. He was as heartily disliked by a number of his officers as Lord Lucan, and was even more arrogant. They also hated each other. Lord Cardigan, first when commanding the 15th Hussars, and later with the 11th Hussars, adopted the same methods as his brother-in-law and with good results: when Major-General Sir Thomas Arbuthnot inspected the 15th Hussars, he warmly congratulated Lord Cardigan on their appearance and performance. Like Lord Lucan, however, Cardigan believed that loyalty and discipline were imperative in a regiment; and there was a clique of his officers who were uncooperative. These were usually middle-class professionals who had seen service in India, and were 'great men in their own estimation'. They considered their aristocratic commanders ignorant fools unversed in war, which was not strictly correct, for Lord Lucan had fought well under the Russians. Admittedly Lord Cardigan had only trained for war by 'riding fearlessly across country with foxhounds in Northamptonshire', but he was certainly brave. Also it is probably wrong to assume that the young progressives with war service – at any rate only in India – really knew better than their superiors, for the command of a few native troops in a colonial war was not really the perfect preparation for war in Europe against Europeans. Even Wellington was spoken of as a mere sepoy general until he proved himself against the French in the Peninsula.

Lucan and Cardigan are usually be-rated for their severe disciplinary methods: court-martialling their officers; flogging their men. It seems that the officers responded less well to their treatment than did the men to theirs; one of the latter, indeed, describes Lord Cardigan as the 'ideal cavalry leader', and others, after the Charge, said to him, 'we are ready to do it again, my Lord'. Both of the noble lords played a major role in the most famous cavalry charge in the history of war; but they did not come out of it with much credit.

If the partial failure of the British at Balaclava belongs to the noble lords, the degree of success achieved must surely be assigned to Sir Colin Campbell. Colin Campbell was born in Glasgow in 1792, the eldest of the four children of John Macliver, a Glasgow carpenter, and his wife Agnes Campbell. The family had gone down in the world, for Colin came of good stock on both sides. His paternal grandfather, Laird of Ardnave in the island of Islay, had been out in the '45 Rebellion, and so forfeited his estate. His mother belonged to a respectable family long settled in Islay, with its chief, the ancestor of the existing Earls of Cawdor. Not a few of Colin's kinsmen had served in the army, and when he was presented to the Duke of York by his mother's brother, Colonel John Campbell, the commander-in-chief promised him a commission, entering him under the name Colin Campbell, thinking him another of that clan. His shrewd uncle told him later that 'Campbell was a name which it would suit him for professional reasons to adopt'; and this he did. Colin Campbell had seen much service by the time he took command of the Highland Brigade in the Crimea. He had been on the Walcheren expedition in 1809, served through the Peninsular War, and was wounded at the siege of San Sebastian. He took part in the expedition to the United States in 1814, and then passed nearly thirty years in garrison duty at Gibraltar, Barbados, Demerara and other places. In 1837 he took over command of the 98th, and for his brilliant services in the Second Sikh War, 1848-9, he was made a K.C.B., thereafter commanding for three years at Peshawar against the frontier tribes. At Balaclava he was at his best. Given the task of guarding Balaclava, he made every effort to render it safe. During the battle he was ubiquitous; and he defended Balaclava in person at the head of the 93rd at the most critical hour.

EN ROUTE

EN ROUTE

*'Russian soldier: "Why is it, sir, they stand up for the
Turks and their wickedness?"*
*Captain Ermalaev: "You see, my lads, the Turkish
Sultan has promised the English a piece of his
land." '*

HODASEVICH

Since 1740 France had enjoyed a treaty right to the custody of the
Holy Places in and near Jerusalem, which were the subject of
pilgrimage to the devout of both the Roman Catholic and Greek
Orthodox Churches. But for more than a hundred years France
had done little or nothing to carry out her duties, and during this
period of neglect, members of the Greek Orthodox Church, with
the permission of the Sultan of Turkey, occupied and repaired the
shrines which France had allowed to fall into decay.

In 1850, however, Louis Napoleon, soon to become Emperor
Napoleon III, anxious to conciliate Roman Catholic sentiment in
France, renewed the claim and succeeded in getting substantial
Turkish recognition. Russia then supported the Greek Church
and protested strongly; and the Turkish Government, finding that
it could not conciliate France without incurring the hostility of
Russia, tried unsuccessfully to concede something to both.

The dispute was aggravated by Tsar Nicholas's personal dis-
like of the new French Emperor whom he looked upon as an
upstart, and by the fact that he had ideas on the future of the
Turkish Empire of which Napoleon did not approve – a dis-
approval shared, in part, by Britain and Austria, the other
European Great Powers. Tsar Nicholas classed Turkey as 'the
sick Man of Europe'. The Turk, so he said, was very ill. It would be
a grave misfortune if Russia and England were not to provide
beforehand for the contingency of his death. In conversation
about the matter through the British Ambassador in Russia, the
Tsar stated that although he did not want to see Constantinople
in the occupation of Russia, or of any Great Power, he believed
that Bulgaria, Serbia and other Turkish provinces should be made
independent and put under the protection of Russia. England

9

Tsar Nicholas

might ensure her communication with India and the East, which passed through Turkish-controlled areas, by occupying Egypt and Crete.

The British Government would not agree to this. They did not think the end of Turkey was so near as the Tsar supposed, and in any case, should the catastrophe come and Turkey show herself incapable of maintaining law and order throughout her large empire, then her future should be regulated at a congress between Russia, Britain, France and the leader of the Germanic powers, Austria.

Convinced in his own mind that Turkey could not survive, Tsar Nicholas took a step calculated to hasten the end. In the spring of 1853 he sent Prince Mentschikoff on a mission to Constantinople to ask formally, though leaving on one side control of the Holy Places, that the Greek Orthodox Church in Turkey might be placed under the protection of Russia. From a

Russian point of view there was something to be said for this demand. It expanded a principle laid down by treaty eighty years before when the Greek Orthodox Church in Constantinople had been placed under Russian protection; and it accorded to Russia a right similar to that which Austria already held of protecting the members of the Roman Catholic Church. But the members of the Roman Church were few, those of the Greek Church were many; and Lord Stratford de Redcliffe, Britain's Ambassador in Turkey, thought that this might give Russia a right of intervention in almost every Turkish province. Lord Stratford accordingly persuaded the Turkish Government to reject courteously but firmly the Russian proposal.

In consequence of Turkey's refusal, Russia occupied with her armies the Turkish-controlled lower Danubian provinces which lay on their common frontier, and Britain and France, as Turkey's supporters, took the precaution of sending their fleets to the mouth of the Dardanelles, although attempts by diplomacy were continued to try to prevent a complete rupture. Austria was interested in the free navigation of the Danube, and as the river reached the sea in the area now occupied by the Russian forces, she added her efforts to those of Britain and France to settle the dispute.

The suggestions for compromise put forward by the Powers met with a better response from Russia than from Turkey; but subsequent events precluded any hope of a peaceful solution. When the Sultan called on Russia to withdraw her troops, she refused so adamantly that it was tantamount to a declaration of war; and the Turkish Army under Omar Pasha crossed the Danube to confront the enemy. Then, on 30 November 1853, a Turkish squadron sailing east from Constantinople across the Black Sea was attacked off Sinope by the main Russian fleet and virtually destroyed. When the news of the massacre at Sinope reached London and Paris, it was received in both capitals with the same feeling of indignation. Few asked whether it was justified, although it was probably Russia's answer to Britain and France for beginning to pass their fleets through the Dardanelles, and the Tsar wanting to strike at the Turkish navy before the Allied ships arrived to help. However, Russia's action, justified or unjustified, destroyed the last chance of peace.

France was already bellicose. In Britain there were two parties in the British Cabinet. Both factions sincerely wanted peace; but their methods for maintaining it were radically opposed. The Prime Minister, Lord Aberdeen, and his immediate friends

11

believed in the good faith of Tsar Nicholas and had little confidence in Turkey. Lord Palmerston, on the contrary, had no faith in Russia but a strong belief in the possible regeneration of the Turkish Empire. Lord Aberdeen thought that peace could be preserved by endeavouring to meet what was reasonable in the demands of Russia. Lord Palmerston thought that it was to be secured only by convincing Russia that if war broke out she would have to deal with more than Turkey. If Lord Aberdeen had stood alone, he might have averted war by conciliation. If Lord Palmerston had stood alone, he might have averted war by action. But Lord Palmerston's action robbed Lord Aberdeen's conciliation of its grace; and Lord Aberdeen's conciliation took the strength out of Lord Palmerston's action. The different opinions in the Cabinet and contrary counsels which reached him gave Lord Stratford, the British Ambassador, his opportunity. Like Lord Palmerston he believed in Turkey and was determined to prevent Russian intervention.

Lord Palmerston

A last attempt at diplomacy not unnaturally failed because the new suggestions at compromise were presented just at the same moment that the Allied navies were entering the Black Sea and their leaders were asking the Russian ships to return to base at Sebastopol. Tsar Nicholas was so deeply offended that he refused even to reply to the new proposals.

The first object was to clear the Russian armies out of the Danubian provinces; and in this Austria was more interested than either Britain or France. Austria offered to join with them and send a Note to Russia requiring evacuation by a fixed date. But the indignation of the British public at the massacre at Sinope was so great that the British Government were unable to resist its demand for war. On 27 March 1854, without waiting for a formal arrangement with Austria, Britain and France addressed an ultimatum to Russia. On the Tsar refusing to reply, they declared war; and very soon afterwards soldiers from Russia, from France and from Britain began moving off on their way to the Crimea.

There were already Russian armies in the Danubian provinces; but on the declaration of war by France and Britain in March 1854, troops began to move towards the Crimea and into Sebastopol. Among these was the Russian Sixth Corps which included the Taroutine Regiment in which Captain Hodasevich served. On 22 April they reached Simpheropol, the chief town of the Crimea and seat of local government. Here through the good offices of the Colonel of the Regiment, Major-General Volkhoff, they were entertained by the inhabitants for two days. On Easter Sunday, 23 April, the troops attended a religious service on the boulevard conducted with all the pomp of the Greek Church, and afterwards each man received two glasses of vodka, a piece of white bread and a pound and a half of beef, the whole being presented by the inhabitants – voluntarily or involuntarily, it is not known. In every Russian regiment a number of men with good voices formed a regimental chorus, and in the evening the band and chorus of the Taroutine Regiment played and sang on the boulevard to the delight of the inhabitants who had, *nolens volens*, so liberally contributed to the soldiers' dinner that day. Captain Hodasevich records a conversation heard on the boulevard which indicates what Russians felt about the war, and their opponents, at the time.

Captain Ermalaev was saying: 'the English go and come on the sea; but there is little chance of them reaching Sebastopol; they would be afraid to; let them try and fight us on land and we would

13

soon see them off. The French we know can fight; but the English, pshaw! They are only used to fighting savages in a far-off country – there, I can't think of the name of it! You must all know. It is the place we were to have gone to by way of the Caucasus if we had not been ordered here. There, I have it on the tip of my tongue! Do you know, Ivanov?'

'I think you mean India,' replied Ivanov.

'Yes, that's it,' caught up Ermalaev.

A number of men had by this time gathered round the two officers; and Ermalaev turned to them and said, 'Well, my lads, do you think we shall beat the French and English?'

'Yes, sir. If they really do come here, we'll show them what we are made of.'

'That's right, my lads! You know, all this business is because these Christians stand up for the dog of a Turk who impales and boils our brethren.'

'Yes, sir. But why is it they stand up for the Turks and their wickedness?'

'Why, my lads? You see the Turkish Sultan has promised the English a piece of his land, and they will do anything for more colonies although they already possess so many.'

From Simpheropol the Russians moved on to Bakschi Serai, half-way to Sebastopol, and reached it late in the evening after a tiring march. The inhabitants were mainly Tartars who lived in oriental-type houses of one storey built round courtyards opening on narrow dirty streets. The most notable building was the palace of the ancient Khans which at the beginning of the war had been turned into a military hospital. This was the scene of the Russian poet Pushkin's beautiful poem 'The Fountain of Bakschi Serai' which he wrote in 1826. The Tartars were not very friendly; and the regiment was not as well received by them as by the inhabitants of Simpheropol. But the next day, they left Bakschi Serai for Sebastopol, which they reached after two days' march; and so their long trek from Nijni Novgorod in the centre of Russia came to an end.

The Taroutine Regiment, at first, occupied the barracks at Alexander, east of Man-of-War harbour (see map 4, page 96); but later they moved to Fort Nicholas and finally to the area of the Théâtre in the south-west of the city. Captain Hodasevich was surprised at the large number of guns at Sebastopol and learnt that it was because the town was the storehouse for the Crimea and the forts of the eastern coast of the Black Sea, and conse-

14

quently all the old guns from the Caucasus were sent to Sebastopol, as well as those from the different stations in the Crimea. The
guns that could be repaired were returned to the forts to which
they belonged after being put in order, while those which were
almost worn-out were put in store. Another reason for the number
of guns in the town was that the ships of the Black Sea fleet were
built and armed at Nickolayeff nearby and brought to Sebastopol;
and when they were broken up, their guns were placed in store.
The result was that for seventy years the number of guns had
increased to something enormous. Captain Hodasevich has something also to say about the numbers of men available to man the
town's defences. The 7,000 convicts housed there had been immediately put to work on the fortifications by Prince Mentschikoff, and there were upwards of 25,000 dockers and sailors of the
Black Sea Fleet soon to be organized by Admiral Korniloff. The
strength of the army he gives as 26,000; most of whom were
infantry.

*Le capitaine d'état-major Henri Loizillon attaché à la division du
général Brunet* was at Versailles when war was declared, and later
he was posted to Marseilles before moving to the Crimea. Judging
from the letters he wrote to his parents, the French army was as
eager for the fray as the Russians. He says that all the officers
hoped to be sent out to the Crimea and were doing all they could
to get posted there. It would be shameful if he did not manage to
get there too! If they feared for his life, they must remember that it
was not possible to gain glory without taking risks, and that they
could reassure themselves that he had every confidence in himself
et en son étoile. He never gave a thought about being wounded or
killed, nor did any of the others on the way to the east. Besides, he
was going in the best possible circumstances, for General Brunet
whom he served as *état-major* was both charming and helpful, as
were his senior staff-officers. But *le capitaine* was in a reserve
division and, as it turned out, he had to wait a long while before
he was posted to the Crimea.

British troops were also leaving their peacetime stations to con-
verge on Portsmouth or Plymouth to take ship on their way to the
Black Sea. The Guards started off from Buckingham Palace, and
the Queen and Prince Albert with their children came out on to
the balcony to say good-bye. When they cheered her, the Queen
seemed much affected and graciously waved as they marched
away.

15

The Guards cheer the Queen prior to leaving for the Crimea

Generally speaking the embarkation had the gay informality of a picnic, at any rate for the officers. Cases of wine, baskets of hot-house fruit, and bouquets of flowers were handed up the sides of the transports, and the general hope was that the war would not be over before they arrived.

For the cavalry and artillery, however, a pleasant voyage was not in store. The transport of horses presents great difficulties; horses are bad sailors and suffer severely from confinement at sea. To make matters worse sailing ships were chosen for them instead of steamers and this increased their passage to nearly seventy days. They had a particularly rough time in the Bay of Biscay. As the vessel rolled from side to side, it pitched all the horses forward off their feet against the mangers. The animals then got absolutely frantic, stamping and screaming; and this mingled with the shouts of the men trying to pacify them created complete bedlam. Some got themselves into a most critical position with their bodies underneath other horses who were kicking and plunging; and to get them out was a dangerous and difficult affair. The soldiers did all they could, and were ably seconded by the sailors, but several horses broke their legs and had to be shot and thrown overboard.

Napoleon III

Meanwhile, Lord Cardigan, by permission of the commander-in-chief, travelled independently of his brigade to the seat of war. Accompanied by his A.D.C., he left London for Paris on 8 May 1854, gave a dinner-party at the Café de Paris on the 10th, was entertained by Napoleon III and the Empress Eugénie at the Tuileries on the 11th, and left Marseilles in a French steamer on the 16th. On 21 May he arrived at the Piraeus, spent a couple of days sightseeing in Athens, and then on 24 May anchored off Scutari and went ashore to report to Lord Lucan, 'looking as usual highly important'. Later, on 13 October, his yacht *Dryad* arrived in Balaclava harbour. It had been brought out from England with his French chef aboard by his great friend Hubert de Burgh. Mr. de Burgh landed, went to Lord Cardigan's tent and was greatly distressed to find him dining off some soup in a jug and boiled salt pork. From that day, however, Lord Cardigan by permission of Lord Raglan dined, and often slept, aboard.

Captain Ewart of the 93rd Sutherland Highlanders was caught unawares by the war with Russia. Quite unconcerned, he had gone off with his parents to St. Leonards to stay with an aunt who was recovering from a serious illness, when on 11 February 1854 a report reached him to the effect that several regiments had been placed under orders for Turkey. He suggested to his father that it would be best for him to start immediately for London to find out if the rumour were true; and they both agreed that if the 93rd had been ordered on active service he should go back instantly to Plymouth where they were stationed in the Citadel. Therefore, after saying good-bye to his mother and aunt, he drove to the station accompanied by his father, meaning to return in the evening if the report proved to be unfounded. There was, of course, the possibility of his being obliged to rejoin without coming back – and their parting was 'tinged with sadness'. His father, however, was too good a soldier to wish him to delay if duty called, so they shook hands and Captain Ewart jumped into the train. Alas! It was the last time he was to see his father – who died soon afterwards. On arrival in London he found that not only had several regiments been placed under orders for active service, but that his own would be one of the first to embark. After buying some things likely to be useful, he left London for Plymouth.

Only a few days earlier his brother Charles of the Royal Engineers had received a sudden order to accompany General Burgoyne to Turkey, and he had accordingly left for Constantinople *via* Paris and Marseilles; his eldest brother Frederick, commanding the *Trafalgar*, a three decker, had already entered the Black Sea with the combined fleets; a cousin, Salisbury Ewart, was serving in the 93rd, so the Ewart family was very well represented in the Crimean War.

The 93rd had received instructions to leave behind all weakly men; and on reaching Plymouth, Ewart was sent for by Lieutenant-Colonel Ainslie and asked if he would have any objection to remaining at home in command of the depôt, as they wanted to appoint an officer in whom they had confidence. Ewart replied that if he were offered a thousand pounds he would still decline to remain at home when the regiment had been ordered on active service, and he sincerely hoped the Colonel would choose someone else.

A few days previous to leaving England the regiment was inspected on the Hoe by Major-General Sir Harry Smith.[1] Private

1. *As a young officer in the Rifle Brigade Harry Smith was present at the capture of Badajoz in 1812. When the British troops got out of hand and sacked the town, he stood guard over a beautiful Spanish girl and rescued her from the mob. Later he married her and took his 'Spanish Bride' with him on his campaigns. From 1848–52 he was Governor of Cape Colony; and Ladysmith in Natal was named after his wife.*

George Greig wrote in his diary that the 93rd were first reviewed by General Smith and afterwards formed up in square to hear the following address:

'Highlanders, you will on Monday embark for the purpose of meeting the enemies of your Country. Soldiers have nothing to do with the cause of quarrels, their duty is to fight; but in this instance you have a noble cause to fight for, the protection of the weak by the strong. You will be led by Lord Raglan, a man who was at the right hand of the Duke of Wellington, a man who knows how to lead you to victory as well as you know how to fight to obtain it. One thing I want to impress upon your minds, and that is to be good comrades with your gallant allies the French. I say "gallant" most truly for they were once our foes, and we know their worth. I never met a British Regiment that would not fight. I know you will. Colonel Ainslie, I wish you and these Highlanders every success.'

The 93rd embarked aboard the *Himalaya*. This was the largest steamer of the period and carried two companies of Rifles and some engineers besides the Highlanders, making, with the crew, 1,542. The 93rd had been brought up to strength by 150 volunteers from the 42nd (Black Watch) and 79th (Cameron Highlanders); and, according to Captain Ewart, were 'a thousand very fine set of fellows, as splendid looking soldiers as could be found in the world, imbued with a magnificent spirit, and ready to go anywhere and do anything'. The 93rd had a good reputation at this time. Raised in 1799, they were originally from Sutherland, with a few from Ross and the neighbouring counties. The first recruiting was conducted under the immediate supervision of the Sutherland family. A census having been carried out on the extensive estates of the Countess of Sutherland, her agents required a proportion of the able-bodied sons of her tenantry to join the Sutherland Regiment 'as a test of their duty to their feudal chief and sovereign'. This is said to have been the last time feudal power was used on a large scale in the Highlands. The men came willingly and were of the highest character. Grouped by parishes, there grew up a healthy rivalry between the townships; and the men did not like bringing dishonour upon their own particular parishes by behaving badly. They were warned that anyone committing a serious offence would have his name written up in the porch of the local kirk for all to see – Sir Colin Campbell was to threaten them with this at Alma later. Although the original narrow local recruitment was not maintained over the years the early high standards of behaviour lingered on. When many regiments were renowned for drunkenness and disorderly conduct, the 93rd maintained a slightly higher tone; and they were 'hot and fiery' fighters into the bargain. In the Crimea the 93rd still had more Gaelic-speaking men than the other Highland regiments. In 1850–1 there had been so many who could not understand English that fourpence a day as extra pay had been sanctioned to four corporals to drill the regiment and explain in Gaelic the English words of command.

After passing Gibraltar in three days fifteen hours, they reached Malta on 7 March, and disembarked. Enlivened by soldiers from the various regiments encamped on the island, Valetta was a gay-looking place. The number of priests and barefooted monks to be seen in the streets was quite extraordinary; and one of the sights was a monastery where the baked bodies of deceased monks were on show to the public. Since the site chosen for the 93rd's encampment was also a cemetery, they preferred, however, to spend their time studying young ladies who were alive!

On 23 March, 800 troops under Generals Canrobert and Bosquet sailed into Valetta harbour; and their vessel was cheered in by British troops on the quays, while the French lined their ship's rails and returned the compliment. Later the French generals carefully inspected the Guards, the 93rd and the Rifle Brigade, and were delighted with what they saw, being especially struck by the appearance of the Highlanders. Then they asked to see how the British received cavalry in square. When squares were duly formed, General Canrobert rode into one, the men making way for him to pass. As he did so, he took off his cocked hat and said courteously with a bow, 'It is only by permission that a French officer ever enters a British square.' Later some Chasseurs officers came to breakfast, and insisted on trying on Highland bonnets.

On 6 March the 93rd embarked on board the *Kangaroo*. Bands played them down to the quay and the regiments left behind cheered. Then they set sail for Gallipoli. They had an agreeable passage, finding the Greek islands 'most interesting'; and they saw the site of ancient Troy, which brought back for Captain Ewart, whose account is followed here, schoolboy memories of the *Aeneid*. It was nearly eleven when they entered the Dardanelles; but by hoisting the recognized night-signal, they escaped being fired on. The moon was shining brightly so they had a good view of the rather barren lands on both sides of the Straits as they glided through. They reached Gallipoli on 6 April 1854, disembarked the same evening, and marched a short distance to

General Canrobert

camp, which was for the first night in a Turkish graveyard, but moved next day to a more salubrious spot.

When going down the side of *Kangaroo* something caught Captain Ewart's scabbard, tipped it, and the handle of his claymore being heavy, it slipped out into the deep water of the Dardanelles where it was quite impossible to recover, so he borrowed a sword from one of the drummers, and sent off immediately a letter home to ask his family to send out another one.

The weather at Gallipoli was unpleasant with bitter winds and hailstorms; and the 93rd lost two men early in their stay because of it. Captain Ewart's piper with a friend went one night to Gallipoli three miles away. The following morning a drummer rushed into his tent with the sad news that they had been found dead on the road. They had drunk too much of some horrible stuff called *aqua ardente* sold by the Greeks; and the intense cold brought on apoplexy which killed them. The 93rd got some wood from Gallipoli and built rough coffins which they covered with tartan plaids. Then they buried them side by side in a deep grave on a hill overlooking the Dardanelles, where the cairn to their memory could be seen by ships passing through the Straits.

It was amusing to see the systematic manner in which the French took possession of Gallipoli, even going so far as to name all the streets. The Turks seemed to care very little what was done, and just sat as usual cross-legged on a counter in front of their shops, smoking their hubble-bubble pipes and apparently resigned to their fate. Ewart learnt a few words of Turkish; but there was little to buy, the general answer being 'Yok Johnny' meaning no. For a period they went off into the interior to dig two miles of trenches across the narrowest part of the peninsula from Bulair to the Dardanelles. Out in the country there was more to be had; and they were able to buy figs, and sometimes bread and eggs.

Zouaves

Taken with the daily rum ration, this brought something like contentment, although the digging was hard work. Among the white tents of the Rifles nearby, they noticed a large green tent. This was said to belong to Lady Erroll who had come to the war with her husband. They asked if they could grow beards while working on the fortifications, but Sir George Brown would not allow even moustaches and ordered some of the officers to clip back their whiskers.

On 28 April 1854 Lord Raglan arrived at Gallipoli; but went on the same evening to Constantinople. The next day Prince Napoleon landed with some troops, bringing up the French force to 25,000; but they still had no cavalry. Of the various regiments, the Chasseurs de Vincennes and the Zouaves appeared to Ewart much the best, the latter looking particularly strong and muscular, and, though not tall, up to anything. They offered the English a taste of absinthe, but it was not to their liking. Some soldiers changed clothes, and one night a Highlander came back to camp dressed as a Zouave. How the Frenchman got on with the kilt he received in exchange, they never heard. Highlanders and Zouaves started walking about arm in arm, sometimes four or five abreast singing 'Auld lang syne' and 'Mourir pour la patrie'. Of course they could not understand each other; but the words 'Russes no bon' seemed to make everything all right. On 6 May the 93rd embarked from Gallipoli on the *Golden Fleece* with Sir George Brown also on board. It was a lovely night and the Sea of Marmara was like a sheet of glass. They had already learnt that their next stop was the Turkish capital Constantinople and were pleased to be leaving Gallipoli.

Captain Ewart was on deck the moment it was light, and was never to forget the glorious scene as they approached the Bosphorus, or the first sight of Constantinople, with its mosques and minarets. The 93rd were housed in a corridor of the mighty barrack at Scutari which was to become the General Hospital and scene of Florence Nightingale's activities. They were met at Scutari by Sir Colin Campbell who had arrived to command the Highland Brigade. As there was no place for the officers of the 93rd in the barracks, Sir Colin allowed them to use two of his rooms with mats on the floor to sleep on.

A magnificent ball, given by the French Ambassador, was being held in Constantinople on the first night of their arrival. The colonel and four officers from each regiment were invited, and being one of the four seniors in the 93rd, Captain Ewart was

Lord Stratford de Redcliffe

included. Putting his best coat and buckle shoes into a carpet bag and borrowing a claymore he crossed the Bosphorus with a brother officer in a Turkish caïque *en route* for the ball. Nothing could have exceeded the astonishment of the Turks as they jumped ashore in their kilts and large Highland bonnets, the first seen in Constantinople. Porters fought for the honour of carrying their bags, and a large admiring crowd followed them to their hotel.

The ball was a wonderful sight, about fifteen hundred people being present including all the ambassadors – except Lord Stratford de Redcliffe who was ill – and innumerable Turkish pashas whose coats were a mass of gold lace. St. Arnaud looked well in his marshal's uniform covered with embroidery and decorations, and all the British generals were there. Prince Napoleon was dressed like the great Napoleon, and with the

24

family likeness it seemed the ancient enemy was among them again. Near Captain Ewart was a group consisting of the Prince, the French Ambassador, Lord Raglan, Lord Lucan, Sir Colin Campbell, Sir George Brown and a good-looking officer who was said to have some sort of claim to the throne of Poland. It was a brilliant scene, and one not easily forgotten. The Turks, usually apathetic, showed great interest in the Highland dress; and the officers of the 93rd were surrounded by them the whole evening. One insisted on examining Ewart's claymore and was intrigued by the badger's head on his sporran. A French general, however, told him that kilts would be of no use in Algeria where the bushes were thick and thorny. Three little Turkish boys were at the ball dressed in uniform. One of them, they were told, was to marry a daughter of the Sultan. Although the men outnumbered the women, and there were only a few pretty faces, the supper was excellent, and there was plenty of champagne.

On 11 May the Duke of Cambridge arrived. He immediately rode up and inspected the Guards and 93rd, and said he was very pleased to find that he was to command them. They were equally

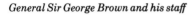

General Sir George Brown and his staff

proud to be under a general who was a cousin of their Queen – and also not sorry to part company with Sir George Brown!

When the ground dried out, the 93rd moved from the huge barrack to a camp on the Turkish burial ground known as Cyprus Grove. It was infested by dogs which did nothing but bark and howl and fight all night long. The noise was so horrible that several were shot by officers with their revolvers. One day Ewart and a friend paid a visit to the Sweet Waters of Europe, a Constantinople show place on the Stamboul side of the Bosphorus, five miles away. They crossed from Scutari in a caïque and found hundreds of Turkish women there eating sweetmeats and enjoying themselves. They all had their faces covered with a sort of gauze, except the eyes and nose, so it was difficult to make out their features; but several seemed pretty, and they all had fine eyes. In one corner were a group of French girls giggling happily together. There were several bands, and dancing girls performed from time to time between the singing. Not far from Sweet Waters they came suddenly upon the whole of the Sultan's wives. They were in carriages escorted by a number of tall black fellows with drawn swords. The procession passed slowly, and some of the young

Captain Ewart's wanderings

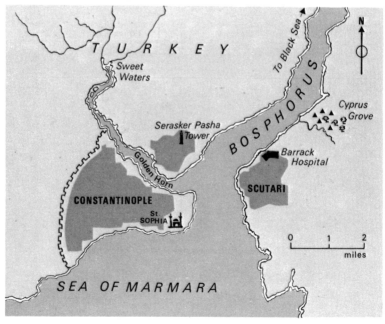

26

ladies laughed heartily at the kilts. One who had her face and neck uncovered was exceedingly good-looking.

Captain Ewart visited the Serasker Pasha Tower, the highest in Constantinople. This afforded a magnificent view over the Bosphorus, the Sea of Marmara and the distant mountains of Asia. He also went round the town itself. The streets were 'so excessively narrow, dirty and ill-paved that walking was anything but pleasant'; but there was plenty to amuse in the bazaars, where soldiers could get drunk for sixpence or syphilis for a shilling; and the officers might perhaps acquire bargains in gear for the field. There were Turkish women walking around in yellow boots without stockings; and in the doorways old women sat smoking while younger women lay on cushions, their faces not so closely covered, eating sweets, sipping lemonade, and fluttering their henna-tinged eyelids as they smoothed their robes over their large breasts, their dyed nails red against the white silk. Meanwhile, the menfolk were doing all they possibly could to cheat the bargain hunters, asking for everything about twenty times what they would take. Ewart found it was the safest plan to get hold of a sharp Turkish boy to 'cheapen' for him. In this way he picked up a second baggage

Constantinople

animal at a sale that was going on, and invested in a couple of good saddle-bags.

A magnificent palace was being built for the Sultan outside Constantinople, and it was said that he took a great deal more interest in it than he did in the war. It was nearly finished, and Ewart was struck by the luxury of the bath prepared for the ladies of the harem; it was a very large marble one, with beautiful cushions all round.

The principal sight at Constantinople was the Mosque of St. Sophia which no Christian could enter without the special permission of the Sultan. One day when Ewart was passing the mosque on his own, the thought occurred to him that 'money did everything in England and might be equally powerful in Turkey'. Much wishing to see the inside of the celebrated mosque, he accordingly knocked quietly at the large door. As soon as it was opened, he made signs that he wanted to enter; but the beadle at once ordered him off. Having pulled out his purse, he tendered first one coin and then another, but each time the beadle shook his head. At last he increased the sum so much that he noticed a change in the man's countenance, who then, looking stealthily round, beckoned him in. There was a second large door farther on, and as they approached it, the man seized Captain Ewart's arm and hurried him up a staircase to a sort of gallery where the man left him, locking the door behind him. Ewart found that from the gallery he could see the whole interior of the mosque, which was 'tolerably well filled with people standing or sitting in groups', some listening attentively to men who were reading the Koran. After gazing down on the scene for some time, he began to wonder what had become of the beadle, as he had no wish to pass the night in the gallery. Presently he heard footsteps and back the man came, locking the door again as he did so. Ewart at once made signs that he had seen enough, and wished to go out, upon which the rascal demanded more money. Having already paid him handsomely, Ewart was quite determined not to give him any more, and approached the door. The beadle instantly placed himself against it, and Ewart saw he was a prisoner. He had no claymore, but was dressed in his kilt and shell jacket with his dirk at his side; the latter the man had evidently not noticed. He was an ill-looking fellow and sturdy, but Ewart felt sure he could frighten him, so suddenly pulling out his dirk he pointed it at the man's throat putting on as he did so a most ferocious look. Instantly the man turned, unlocked the door and made his escape. Ewart was after him in a moment, and, opening the large outer door by which he

28

had entered, walked triumphantly out, taking care to get away from the mosque as quickly as he could, 'short of being too undignified'.

While at Scutari the 93rd suffered another loss. Between the camp and the landing-place was a small stream over which it was normally easy to step. Two officers, Macnish and Clayhills, crossed it one day and hired a boat and went over to Constantinople. It was dark when they returned, and a heavy rainstorm had made the stream rise very rapidly. In trying to get over, they were both swept off their legs. Clayhills, after being carried along a few yards, managed to catch hold of a bough, and so escaped being drowned. He ran up to the camp and at once gave the alarm, and immediately a search was made for Macnish. No trace of him could be found although the search went on for several days. Later, however, his body was discovered beyond a small bridge, whose culvert looked too small to let a body through, lying face upwards in clear water near the spot where the stream joined the Bosphorus. He had been carried three hundred yards tumbling down the stream but his claymore was still at his side.

On 26 May, the 79th arrived, and on 7 June, the 42nd; Sir Colin Campbell's Highland Brigade was complete. By now the troops had begun embarking; and on 13 June the Highlanders left Turkey for Bulgaria. Their destination was the port of Varna, and the object of the operation was to build up a force to support the Turks who were holding the Russians on the Danube, where the fortress of Silistria was resisting gallantly.

BULGARIA

BULGARIA

'And then on 19 July it was known that a serious epidemic of cholera, prevalent over the south of Europe, had broken out in the French camp. Three days later the British camps were infected. The tents were moved, but the sickness followed them.'

Varna at first sight seemed an attractive place: a little town of dusty squares and minarets enclosed by a white wall beside a sandy bay. The nine-mile valley up to Aladyn, where the troops first encamped, was a rolling orchard countryside with wooded slopes. At first all was contentment. Then in July the serious epidemic of cholera prevalent that summer all over Europe spread from the French camp, and the last few months in Bulgaria were horrible. The men became sickly and weak; many died; all were miserable; discipline went by the board; looting began; and soldiers fearing cholera got dead drunk on the coarse strong brandy they believed was a preventative and lay about covered with flies in the blazing sun. Officers too became lax, slouching about with buttons undone and gauze turbans round their forage caps, bored to death and longing to move.

Like the rest of the army Captain Ewart enjoyed his first weeks in Bulgaria. His brothers in the Navy and Royal Engineers joined the family party; and they had dinner together several times, sometimes ashore, sometimes in the *Arethusa*. Previous to the arrival of the Guards and Highlanders, the Light Division, along with the 8th Hussars and 17th Lancers under Lord Cardigan, had moved up to Aladyn; but the 13th Light Dragoons and 5th Dragoon Guards, one of the few heavy regiments that had arrived, remained near Varna with the First Division. Alongside the British there were French Zouaves and Chasseurs and Turkish troops, the latter consisting of badly mounted Turkish lancers and infantry in brown uniform with white trousers, slow in movement and very dirty, and the music of their bands dismal in the extreme. The combined fleets lay at anchor offshore, and Admiral Dundas commanding the fleet and Admiral Lyons commanding the inshore squadron both visited the camp. The 93rd had a large lake close to

33

where their tents were pitched, and as it seemed full of fish some tried string and bent pins to see what they could catch. On 18 June, the anniversary of Waterloo, the *entente* was sufficiently *cordiale* for the French and English to be seen fishing together happily.

Daily, orders were awaited to advance on Silistria, the fortress on the Danube to the north of them which the Russians were investing and which was holding out so gallantly with the active help of a few volunteer British officers. As no orders arrived, and several officers expressed a wish to see what was happening, two officers per regiment were allowed to go up to Silistria as observers; but for the rest of the army it was a matter of drills, field-days, and boredom relieved later by constant changes of camp sites to get away from the cholera-ridden French, some going as far away as Shumla and Janibazar.

The Duberlys

Lord Lucan and Lord Cardigan though brothers-in-law were hardly on speaking terms; and knowing how they hated each other, Lord Raglan attempted to keep them apart as much as possible. Lord Cardigan, though only a brigade commander, was sent forward to Bulgaria and put in charge of the bulk of the cavalry, and Lord Lucan, the nominal divisional commander, was left fuming and fretting at Scutari completely out of touch with the troops he should have been leading. He was separated from his division more than 150 miles away across the Black Sea with no orders and nothing to do except watch transport after transport going off to Varna, some carrying cavalry regiments to swell Lord Cardigan's command. Lord Raglan, meanwhile, also at Varna, dealt directly with Lord Cardigan, seemingly encouraging him deliberately to go over his immediate superior's head.

Lord Lucan's patience finally gave way. He wrote a firm letter to Lord Raglan demanding his rights, and sent a stern rebuke to Lord Cardigan. The first insisted on being allowed to come to Varna; the second ordered his brother-in-law to mend his ways, and kindly note that 'as was customary and proper in the Service, all returns and reports were to be sent through his divisional commander.' This brought some results although it left Lord Lucan almost as isolated as before. He was indeed allowed to go to Varna; but by the time he arrived, most of the cavalry had moved on. Cholera was raging, the state of the town was disgusting, and the Light Brigade and Horse Artillery had gone off to Devna nine miles away. Also, no one was expecting Lord Lucan at Varna, and only the 5th Dragoon Guards remained behind at his disposal.

Mrs. Duberly by persistent pressure in the right places had now managed to reach the seat of war with her husband and their five horses, and in Bulgaria Captain Duberly provided for her a double marquee, cool in the heat and warm at night – 'our pretty marquee and green bower', she called it. With their arabas (carts), a fine stud and appropriate staff, they had a well constituted open-air household; and she made friends with Lady Erroll, whose husband was in the Rifles; and visited Mrs. Cresswell, wife of an officer of the 11th Hussars, whom she pitied 'for the unnecessary discomforts in which she was living'. She described their camp at Devna as most picturesque: in the midst of a fertile plain, near a sparkling river and carpeted with brilliant flowers: burrage, roses, larkspur, heather and a lovely flower the name of which she did not know. She and Henry wandered among the hills on the first afternoon at Devna, and Bob 'sped over the long grass and

35

delicate convolvulus neighing with delight on being released from his picket-rope'. When Henry rode down to Varna to collect the pay from the commissariat chest, Mrs. Duberly went to meet him; and she also rode around the countryside with friends among the officers. For example, accompanied by Captain Hall Dare and Captain Evans of the 23rd, she rode one day to Pravadi, the strongest fortified town in Bulgaria, and bought a damson cheese and some Turkish scarfs. In camp, they lived well on eggs and delicacies bought from the inhabitants; though she does speak of their chicken for dinner being so tough that not even their daily onions could get it down; and of the black bread kneaded on the ground being 'a happy mixture of sand and ants and barley' and so sour that it made her eyes water.

In July, when the allies were expecting at last to do some fighting, despatches arrived from Omar Pasha saying that the siege of Silistria had been raised and that the Russian force of 120,000 men was retreating from the Danubian provinces. The Turkish com-

Omar Pasha

mander had a force based on Shumla and could have called on the British and French, but in fact had done little to help the defenders of Silistria. A few British officers had served in the fortress, and had become the heroes of the siege; also, Colonel Grach, a Prussian officer in the Turkish service, had done good work planning defences; and General Cannon of the Indian Army had taken his brigade of Turkish irregulars into the fortress on his own initiative when it looked like falling.

For a time there had been hard fighting. Prince Paskievitch commanding the Russians and General Schelders in charge of their siege-train had both been killed, and on the allied side, Mussa Pasha, the Turkish garrison commander, and Captain Butler, the most forceful of the volunteers. Eventually, however, the Russian effort flagged, and Tsar Nicholas had ordered a withdrawal.

When the Russian withdrawal started, Lord Raglan sent orders to Lord Cardigan, without informing Lord Lucan, to move north from Devna and make a reconnaissance to discover 'if any of the Russian army were still on this side of the Danube', so with about two hundred men Lord Cardigan moved off to the north. As speed was the main object, only the minimum of supplies was taken; but when they reached the Danube, they discovered that the Russians had already retreated. Lord Cardigan patrolled the south bank of the river as far as Rassova and then turned and visited Silistria, finally returning *via* Shumla back to Devna. Although he gained very little information of any importance, he took a fearful toll of his horses many of which were quite unable to stand the heat and lack of water that the reconnaissance entailed. Mrs. Duberly wrote in her diary that: 'On 11th July Lord Cardigan came in having marched all night; the troops have been to Rassova and Silistria and lived for five days on salt pork; they have shot five horses which dropped from exhaustion on the road; they have brought back an araba full of disabled men and seventy-five horses which will be unfit for work for many months, and some of them never again.'

She was out riding when the stragglers came in; and a piteous sight it was, with men on foot driving and goading on their wretched horses, three or four of which could hardly stir. There seemed to have been much unnecessary suffering. One was lucky – in Mrs. Duberly's view – to have its leg broken by a kick just as it came in, for it was shot and put out of its misery. There was an order that no horse was to be destroyed except for glanders or a broken leg. The net result of Lord Cardigan's patrol, which was

37

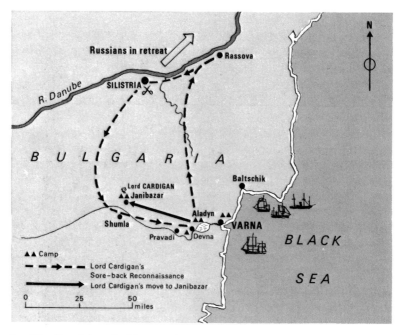

Lord Cardigan's 'sore-back' reconnaissance

called by the army the 'sore-back reconnaissance', was the loss to the Light Brigade of nearly a hundred of its best horses. Lord Cardigan, however, expressed himself satisfied.

To avoid cholera, the Light Division with the Light Brigade were next sent to Janibazar, Lord Lucan again not being consulted about the move of his cavalry. Janibazar was a village on a high barren plateau; but there was a little oasis near the camping site with a spring surrounded by trees and the only shade within miles, and here Lord Cardigan pitched his two large marquees and settled in his staff of cooks, grooms and servants. Protected by the trees from the heat, he was able to make himself comfortable, and he kept in excellent health on a diet of tough meat and champagne.[1]

On 27 July the cholera arrived at Janibazar, and although the cavalry were not affected, sixteen men died in the Rifles, and a few in the Horse Artillery. Back at Varna, however, the 5th Dragoon Guards lost eleven men in two days, so the move may have been

1. A lot of champagne was taken out to the Crimean War. It was believed to have medicinal properties. Captain Ewart's brother in the Navy claimed it cured sick members of his crew.

38

The Siege of Silistria

worthwhile. By August the armies were in a very bad state. The French had already lost thousands from cholera, and many of the British regiments were ravaged. To add to their troubles, on 7 August a furious fire in Varna destroyed thousands of pounds worth of valuable stores including 16,000 pairs of boots and over 150 tons of biscuits. Lord George Paget and the 4th Hussars arrived in Varna about this time. He claimed that the Greeks were at the bottom of the fire. Scattered in colonies throughout the Turkish Empire and south Russia – there was a colony at Balaclava – they hated their Turkish masters and therefore their allies who were not allowed to move about without swords, even when bathing, for fear of them. Lord George records that five Greeks were caught setting fire to buildings by the French, who immediately bayoneted them. He thought 'the French did things better than the British'.

By this time, however, official instructions for Lord Raglan had arrived and a move from Bulgaria became possible. Lord Raglan was told that if he considered it could be undertaken with a reasonable chance of success, he should invest Sebastopol. In a private accompanying letter he was also told that the Emperor of the French had given his blessing to such an enterprise. After a lengthy consultation with General Sir George Brown, his second-in-command, Lord Raglan made the great decision. To the Crimea and on to Sebastopol they would go.

Before, they had seemed stuck, now, with a decision made, events moved fast: a perfect forest of shipping of every kind arrived off the port, and soon Baltschik bay to the north was also crammed. Next the long and difficult task of embarkation began. The order at first was that wives should remain at the camp at Varna; but this did not suit Mrs. Duberly, and she asked the help of Lord Cardigan. In his confident way Lord Cardigan agreed to take up the matter at headquarters, and sought out Lord Raglan to ask permission for Mrs. Duberly to sail with the Fleet. Raglan was a very polite man, a most perfect gentleman, who as Cardigan well knew preferred never to have to utter a definite no. But on this occasion his chivalrous ideals detailed the answer: the shot-torn beaches of the Crimea would be no place for a lady. His reply to Lord Cardigan was a decided negative.

When Fanny heard the sad news, delivered by Lord Cardigan in person, she burst into a passion of tears and collapsed into a chair. Even Lord Cardigan's imperturbability was disturbed at this. He hastened to leave; but as he did so murmured that if she thought proper to disregard the prohibition, he would not try to stop her.

Lord Raglan

Lord Lucan

Reassured, she pulled herself together and started to make plans. She decided she must go down to the quay and get out to the ship disguised as a soldier's wife. She must join the few regimental women who were being allowed to go to the Crimea with their husbands. There was, of course, risk of discovery, for Lord Lucan who commanded the cavalry division was also against her going and would be bound to be watching the embarkation. It could easily end in trouble for her husband and Lord Cardigan, and ignominious banishment for herself.

When the bullock wagons with the soldiers' wives perched on the baggage were drawn up ready, Fanny joined the procession. Wrapped in an old hat and shawl, she clambered up with Henry's help on to their pony's back and followed the wagons down to the quay, masquerading as a soldier's sick wife who had been lent a spare regimental horse. Arrived near the shore, where the danger of recognition was real, they had a long wait facing a bitter wind driving in from the sea. Seeing how Mrs. Duberly was shivering, a soldier's wife gave her another shawl. It was all in vain. When darkness began to fall they were told that embarkation had been postponed until next day. In the morning, in a change of plan, she rode down to the quay on a wagon like the rest of the women. According to her journal, she passed close under Lord Lucan's nose and although he was scanning every face to find traces of a lady, she got through and jumped unobserved down into the baggage boat with Sergeant Connell's wife. The sailors chaffed her, saying her soft skin showed she had not done much work, and that, as sure as anything, she would get a widow's pension. The worst part was leaving the baggage boat and clambering up the ladder aboard the transport. Not being recognised as 'Quality' she received no assistance.

As the embarkation of the troops was progressing, Surgeon Munro of the 93rd arrived at Varna in the *Harbinger*, a vessel carrying General Cathcart and part of the 4th Division. Munro asked to be allowed to contact Dr. Hall, the principal medical officer of the army, so that he might arrange to join his regiment; but the general wished to retain him on his staff and refused his request, saying firmly, 'I intend to keep you, and you must not speak to me on this subject again.'

A few days later while leaning on the rail of the *Harbinger*, Munro recognized Captain Ewart passing in a small rowing-boat under the stern of the ship, and called out to him and explained his predicament. Ewart willingly agreed to tell Colonel Ainslie what was happening to his medical officer, and also, better still, pointed out Dr. Hall's ship about a quarter of a mile away. Then came another stroke of luck. Munro overheard some of his fellow passengers trying to make up a party to man the captain's gig and visit friends in a neighbouring ship. They wanted one more to make up their crew, and Munro's offer to pull an oar was willingly accepted. Having paid their visit, Munro pointed out Dr. Hall's ship, and they agreed to pull over to it. Thus Munro got his interview with the principal medical officer, and received a promise that he could join his regiment the day they landed.

The British fleet of warships and transports sailed from Baltschik Bay on 7 September; but Marshal St. Arnaud, tired of waiting for the British, who had been held up by having to embark their more numerous horses, had already gone ahead. On 8 September Lord Raglan aboard the *Caradoc* reached him at the agreed rendezvous in the middle of the Black Sea. Marshal St. Arnaud was too ill to leave his cabin, and asked the British commander to visit him; but Lord Raglan, with his single arm, could not climb aboard the French three-decker tossing in a rough sea, and sent Admiral Dundas. The admiral found St. Arnaud sitting up in his bunk so ill that he could hardly speak, and tried to discuss the best place to land with Admiral Hamelin instead. They came to no decision, but at length St. Arnaud found strength to say that he would leave it to Lord Raglan.

Next day with General Canrobert, the French second-in-command, Lord Raglan set off aboard the *Caradoc* on a reconnaissance of the Crimean coastline. Approaching the coasts, they saw the domes and cupolas of Sebastopol ahead, and the masts of the ships in the harbour; and they heard church bells ringing. Coming closer, they could see the fortifications were bristling with guns. Steaming north along the coastline, the *Caradoc* ran up the Russian flag, and people rushed down unsuspecting to the beaches to have a closer look. They passed the mouth of the Katcha, but decided it was unsuitable as the beach was narrow and a cluster of tents on the cliffs denoted that it was defended. Steaming farther north, they came to a long sandy beach south of Eupatoria, thirty-five miles north of Sebastopol, where naked men and women were happily bathing together and there were no signs of soldiers. The *Caradoc*'s noisily vibrating engines clattered away into silence. Lord Raglan had found the place he was looking for. He did not invite discussion. He asked a few questions and then announced his decision. This was the place to which the navies must bring the troops to land.

ALMA

ALMA

On the morning of 14 September 1854 the allied fleets and transports arrived off the west coast of the Crimea, and troops began
landing on the shore by Old Fort ten miles south of Eupatoria and
about twenty-five miles north of Sebastopol. The buoy separating
the French and British drifted, and the French, who were quicker
off the mark, occupied the whole beach. The British disembarkation thus had to be made in a new place, and the Rifles landed one
hour after the first French sailors had planted their tricolour in
the sand.

It was a low sandy coast, and at first the only signs of life were a
few mud cottages a mile inshore near which cattle were grazing.
Then a sole Russian officer with a Cossack orderly rode up on
some high ground between the French and English. He dismounted and leisurely surveyed the scene; then, as the troops
landed, he remounted and quietly trotted away. With this solitary
exception no enemy soldiers were seen during the five days of
disembarkation; but local Tartars came in from the villages to
sell fruit and provisions, and the British also bought some carts,
as they were without transport.

During the first night it rained heavily, and the British who
were without tents suffered accordingly. The French had *tentes
d'abri*, and they also took their knapsacks; but the British made
do with great-coats folded flat with a blanket, with shoes, socks
and a forage cap tucked in the folds, and water-bottles and linen
haversacks containing three days' salt pork and biscuit. However,
with weapons and ammunition there was more than enough to
carry. In the 93rd every fifth man took a camp kettle and bill hook.
These were not much use, more of an encumbrance; but Surgeon
Munro later borrowed several kettles to make soup for the
wounded after Alma. 'Fortunately fresh mutton was issued that
evening for the army, otherwise the wounded would not have had

Tartar labourers

any nourishment at all.' The Turks had their bell-type field tents and like the French were never without shelter; but the British army lay out in the open air, with the exception of two nights, until the middle of October when tents were issued through Balaclava.

On the third day the horses were landed. Lord George Paget found it distressing to see them 'as they were upset out of the boats and swimming about in all directions among the ships'. They swam peacefully, but looked rather unhappy with their heads in the air and the surf driving into their mouths. However, only one drowned.

Captain Adye, riding inland with his general to look for water for the artillery horses, found the Rifle Brigade in possession of a large farm. Nearby the French were pillaging and driving off cattle, and remonstrance was of no avail. As Adye left he saw an angry French officer chasing after some of his men and recognized Prince Jerome Napoleon who was commanding the division. The French officers said they could not stop plundering. The spirit of the army was so revolutionary that they had no control over their men; they were much surprised at the discipline of the British troops.

On the fourth day while riding with the Duke of Cambridge who commanded the First Division, Lord George saw Marshal St. Arnaud and thought how different he was from Lord Raglan

46

whom they had just left. The marshal had a staff of twenty: two chasseurs d'Afrique as advance guard, a bodyguard, and an orderly riding close by him carrying a beautiful silk tricolour standard. The Englishmen rode back with him to Lord Raglan who came out to meet them in a mufti coat, and looked, Lord George thought, 'as much less like a commander-in-chief as more like a gentleman'.

From her cabin porthole Mrs. Duberly watched the army disembark; and on 18 September, when all were ashore, it was such a lovely day that she was tempted to go and see her husband. Escorted by the ship's captain, she landed among the artillery on the beach and was told that the 8th Hussars were seven miles inland. After looking round unsuccessfully for a horse to ride, she finally managed to get a lift on a gun-carriage going to the out-posts. Henry was peeping through the tent fly when she drove up, and rushed out, delighted to see her. Shortly afterwards, when she had met the five officers who shared his tent, a patrol of the 13th Light Dragoons came by. These said they had been fired on by a body of 600 Cossacks who were roaming the countryside burning corn and setting fire to villages to deny their use to the allies. Several riflemen, she was told, had been killed by the Cossacks who hovered round the allied armies like a flying cloud. After about an hour in camp, Henry put his regimental saddle on his horse picketed nearby and Mrs. Duberly then mounted and rode back to the shore with her husband and the ship's captain walking on either side along a track 'livid with the glare of vast fires'. The country looked fertile and well cultivated, and in the villages were pleasant-looking houses containing pianos and bookcases and other signs of civilized life. It was nearly dark when they reached the shore and Mrs. Duberly was rowed aboard.

At length, on 19 September 1854, all being ready, the allied armies began their march on Sebastopol. The French, being by the shore, had the advantage of the protection of the navies. Led by skir-mishers they had three divisions in front; then came their fourth division and 7,000 Turks, making, with the baggage guards in the middle, 34,000 men and 68 guns. The British had in the lead the 11th Hussars, the 13th Light Dragoons, I Troop R.H.A. and skirmishers of the Rifle Brigade. The main body had the Light and 2nd Divisions in front followed by the 1st Division (with the 93rd) and 3rd Division. On the flank five miles from the sea were the 8th Hussars, the 17th Lancers and C Troop R.H.A. The rest of the guns were on the right of their divisions in column of batteries; and the baggage, protected by Lord George Paget and the 4th Light Dragoons, brought up the rear. In all there were 27,000 men and 60 guns.

The allied armies marched steadily forward on a front of nearly five miles. The sea breeze had lulled to a breath and the sun shone fiercely down. It was lovely undulating country; and in places the ground was covered with fern and lavender, and some strange herb which no one recognized. Crushed under thousands of heavy boots it gave up a curious smell, strong and bitter. The distant smoke of burning villages and the occasional appearance of a few Cossacks hovering about on the flank were the only evidence that it was enemy country.

There were, however, many weak from cholera and disease, and some of these soon began to fall by the wayside. An occasional shako and mess-tin cast aside was the first sign of trouble. In their innocence Lord George and the rearguard started picking them up. A little farther a man, and then another, were found lying down exhausted, and they used their persuasive powers to make these move on, sometimes with success. This went on gradually increasing until stragglers were lying thick on the ground; and without exaggeration, the last two miles to the Bulganak River resembled a battlefield: men and accoutrements of all sorts lay in such numbers that it was difficult for regiments following to thread their way through. Lady Erroll, bolder than Mrs. Duberly on this occasion, was following her husband in the Rifles on her mule with her French maid on another mule behind her; and the sick men of Lord Erroll's regiment festooned the animals with their rifles.

In the afternoon they began to descend into the wide valley of the Bulganak. By this time water-bottles were empty, and the men were suffering badly, for a breakfast of biscuit and salt pork, and the heat and the marching, had created an intense thirst. On the sight of water, men broke ranks and began to run towards the stream; but Sir Colin Campbell would have none of that with his Highlanders. He stopped them instantly, rated them soundly, and ordered them back to their ranks. Then he sent a detachment forward to fill all the barrels; and in this way they got cleaner water than if they had all rushed into the stream and churned up the mud.

Meanwhile, the Russian cavalry having shown up in some force in the distance, Lord Raglan moved forward with the 8th Hussars and the 17th Lancers under Lord Cardigan to reconnoitre.

48

Suddenly, a Russian horse battery opened fire, and a round shot passed through the English squadrons taking off a man's leg and bounding like a cricket-ball over the heads of Lord Raglan's staff. This was the first shot of the Crimean campaign.

The Russian force was considerable, something like 6,000 infantry and a brigade of cavalry, with nine sotnias or squadrons of Cossacks. Nevertheless the Russian infantry pulled away almost at once, covered by a cloud of skirmishers, and left the cavalry of both sides to a half-hearted skirmish. I and C Troops Royal Horse Artillery were watering their horses when the first shot was heard; and soon afterwards Captain Adye rode up with orders for them to advance and support the cavalry. A smart

Marshal St. Arnaud

gallop over the hilly ground somewhat tried the horses fresh from board ship; but both the 6-pounders and 9-pounders were got over the crest beyond the river in time for the two troops to see the cavalry skirmishing. Support now being at hand, Lord Raglan decided to withdraw the cavalry. With his army on the march, he did not want to bring on a premature general engagement; and retirement by alternate squadrons was begun even before the horse artillery dropped into action. Later C and I Troops were joined by E Battery, and the combined artillery fire was sufficient to cause the Russian cavalry to withdraw and follow their infantry already disappearing from view in the distance. The Light and Second Divisions who on Lord Raglan's orders had by this time manned the crest beyond the river did not advance any farther and were not engaged. Thus ended the 'Affair of the Bulganak'. The British loss was four troopers wounded; the Russians thirty-five.

It was getting dark, and Lord Raglan was anxious to inform the nearest French division under Prince Napoleon what had been happening. As the Prince was a mile away, he asked Colonel Count Lagondie, the attached French officer, to ride over with the news. The colonel was mounted on a strong Flemish mare called Medore, and as he cantered leisurely off the remark was made that if Medore could not be persuaded to move a little faster it would be a long time before Lagondie got back. It was. He never got back at all. Shortsighted, he missed his way and rode into some Russian cavalrymen who made him prisoner. Captain Hodasevich tells of seeing him later being driven off into captivity in a coach.

That night, Marshal St. Arnaud rode up to confer with Lord Raglan at the cottage near the Bulganak which the English commander had made his headquarters. Speaking sometimes in French, sometimes in English, the French general suggested that his army should cross the next river, the Alma, near its mouth and turn the seaboard flank of the Russian army seen lined up in a strong position on the far side; while the English attacked the other Russian flank, caught them in a pincer, and forced them to retire. It was simple, St. Arnaud assured his ally. He took a map from his pocket and put it on the table to demonstrate how easy it would be. The map, drawn with many flourishes of an excited hand, showed the Russians so occupied with the French that they were apparently unaware of the English forces creeping round the rear. The production of the map brought from the marshal a flood of rhetoric, and his eyes glinted feverishly. He was obviously in a high state of animation, probably ill, although apparently not in pain. In a few days he was to die. Lord Raglan sat watching him, listening with a politeness so gravely attentive that those who knew him felt that he was trying not to smile. But he made no comment. Anxious to avoid a strained relationship with the French leader, he thought it better not to risk a discussion which might turn into an argument. After saying that the French could rely on the full cooperation of the British Army, he scarcely spoke another word. He believed that no workable plan could be made until the allies had discovered the full extent of the Russian position. St. Arnaud, however, cannot be blamed for supposing that the principle of his plan had been accepted.

Next day, soon after eleven the two armies moved forward again. The French grumbled at having to wait so long; but the British, being on the flank, had scattered outposts to call in; and in any case were not as brisk and professional at getting on the move as their allies. Behind the cavalry and skirmishers rode Lord Raglan and his staff; and abreast of them were two civilians

Battle of the Alma

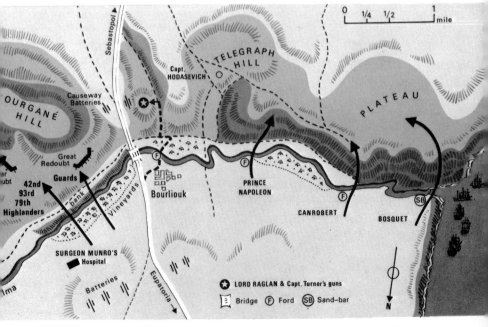

on ponies, one of which, a grey, started neighing and squealing as if the end of the world had come when his stable companion was turned to go to the rear. Lord Raglan said he had never heard a pony make such a noise, and asked who the men were. Journalists, someone suggested. Should they be sent away? Another said it was Mr. Kinglake, the historian, on the grey. Shortly afterwards attention was drawn to Mr. Kinglake again, and even more forcibly. His pony had carted him against his will to the rear after his friend; now it came dashing back, equally out of control, past Lord Raglan and his staff, through the line of skirmishers, and hurled the historian headlong to the ground. They roared with laughter; but when Lord Raglan caught up, he offered Mr. Kinglake one of his own horses, and told his orderly to put the pony's saddle to rights.

By noon they were on the way to the Alma, and Marshal St. Arnaud rode across to confer again. The two leaders met on the crest of a mound on the steppe, and seemed to have an amicable conference. In the silence that followed the halt of the armies behind them, Sir Colin Campbell's men could be heard making ready their cartridges. The noise of the Highlanders clattering their equipment and tearing open their cartridge packets was the only sound which broke an unnatural silence.

The commanders were still on the mound, when Sir George Brown heard Marshal St. Arnaud ask Lord Raglan if he had decided to turn the Russians' flank. But Lord Raglan still did not wish to commit himself until the battle had begun, and the French commander went back to begin his own attack on the Russians' seaboard flank not knowing his ally's plan.

The French took the right of the main road running past Bourliouk village to Sebastopol, and the British the left. The French were faced by steep cliffs and ravines on the far side of the river, while the British had a low wall-like bank to surmount before reaching the gentler slopes up Kourgané Hill. As the Russians believed the cliffs unscalable, the French sector was scantily defended, and the main bulk of the Russian force faced the British.

Behind a cloud of skirmishers the allied order of battle was an échelon from the right. General Bosquet's division led off, marching along the sea-shore with the Turks in the rear. Then came the divisions of General Canrobert and Prince Napoleon, with General Forey in reserve. Next, the English took up the échelon. De Lacy Evans' 2nd Division advanced beside Prince Napoleon; and the Light Division on the left was followed in the second line by the Guards and Highlanders of the 1st Division under the Duke of Cambridge. The other two British divisions were in reserve, one in the rear, the other to the flank with the cavalry.

As the allied armies advanced to the attack, they were able to survey the Russian position. The ground in front of the French sector was lightly manned; and the main enemy body was in position from Telegraph Hill, beside the main road, to Kourgané Hill farther inland. On Kourgané Hill were two partially entrenched redoubts with guns emplaced. It was this hill which the English would have to storm.

It was about noon when the first gun was fired, and Bosquet's brigades crossed the river by a sand-bar near its mouth and began climbing the precipitous slopes, their advance helped by fire from the fleet. The Russians were few in numbers, and the French gained the crest comparatively easily though General Canrobert was slightly wounded. The French divisions crossed the river in succession from the right; General Bosquet's and the Turks near the mouth; Canrobert's and Prince Napoleon's by fords farther inland towards Bourliouk. At Bourliouk there was another ford and the unblown main road bridge; but these were used by the British. The French were delayed because the tracks up the cliffs were too steep for their guns, and they were not willing to fight without artillery support. Almost all Prince Napoleon's division remained on the wrong side of the river under enfilade fire from the Russians; but Bosquet's men were bolder, and a flank movement by them along the crest finally gave the French command of the shore end of the important plateau extending inland to Telegraph and Kourgané Hills.

When the two leading British divisions were about two miles from the Alma, they halted, still in column, to allow stragglers to come up; and Sir Colin Campbell made use of the pause to say a few words to the Highland Brigade. He told them to keep shoulder to shoulder, and when in action, whoever was wounded, of whatever rank, must lie where he fell until the bandsmen came up to attend to him. No soldiers were to go carrying off wounded men. If any soldier did such a thing, he would be in disgrace; his name would be stuck up in his parish church back in Scotland for all to know. Finally he added: 'Don't be in a hurry about firing. Your officers will tell you when it is time to open fire. Be steady. Keep silence. Fire low. Now men, the army is watching us; make me proud of the Highland Brigade!'

Soon after this, the divisions moved forward again; but when

53

they came within range of the enemy guns, they were deployed into line and told to lie down and wait the completion of the French attack. Although English batteries came into action to support them, the enemy guns were more numerous, and in a commanding position, so the English infantry suffered accordingly. For most of them it was their baptism of fire, and they bore it stoically. They picked out the Russian guns and gave them names – Bessie, Maggie and Ann – after unpopular wives of sergeants and officers; they shouted obscene insults at the round shots as they came rushing and bouncing over the plain; they advised their mounted officers which way to ride to avoid them; sometimes, unwary of a shot until too late, they felt the rush of air, and then perhaps heard a sickening thud as a man was hit and the life crushed out of him. At intervals men could be seen all along the line dragging still-quivering bodies to lay them down in the rear of the ranks, and then returning to the front to lie down themselves once more and wait.

Then, urgent messages having been received from the French, it was apparent that the moment for action had at last arrived, and Lord Raglan gave the order for the advance of his whole army. The village of Bourliouk in front of de Lacy Evans' 2nd Division was set on fire by the Russians, and this led to the temporary separation of his two brigades, one passing on either side. It caused some confusion in the British front line. De Lacy Evans' left battalions overlapped and tangled with Sir George Brown's. As a result the Duke of Cambridge's 1st Division was brought forward and stretched, the Guards on the right, the Highlanders on the left, to cover in the second line the two divisions in front.

As it went over the Alma just by Bourliouk the main road to Sebastopol was dominated by Russian batteries stretched across it on the slope, and enfiladed from the guns of the Great Redoubt on Kourgané Hill; and Lord Raglan, having given his general order to advance, veered off towards the right of the burning village on the French side of the road to reconnoitre. Finding a ford, and a ravine leading from it beyond the river, he led his staff up the slope of Telegraph Hill well into enemy territory; but fortunately for him the Russian troops down by the river had been withdrawn. In riding through the outskirts of the village they noticed the body of Lieutenant Cockerell, a young officer of artillery, who with his horse had just been killed by a round shot from the heights. As they reached the river, and crossed by the ford, a sharp skirmish was going on between the Russian outposts and the Zouaves of Prince Napoleon's division on their right. At that moment, one of Lord Raglan's A.D.C.s fell from his horse shot through the shoulder, and was laid under the bank on the opposite side of the river. At the same time the horse of another officer was killed by a bullet in the head.

Lord Raglan summed up the situation in an instant. 'If they can enfilade us,' he said, 'we can certainly do the same to them. Order up Captain Turner and G Battery!'

Lord Raglan pressed on, and passing some French skirmishers in vineyards just beyond the river, soon reached higher ground on the slopes of Telegraph Hill from which in a sort of natural amphitheatre he was able to look across at his divisions crossing the river and approaching the Russians massed on Kourgané Hill. He saw also the heavy Russian guns firing from the Great Redoubt on Kourgané, and a battery of field-guns in the Lesser Redoubt farther away and higher up the hill. Below him was the main road to Sebastopol, with the Causeway batteries guarding it; and to his right, higher up the slope, was the summit of Telegraph Hill. This was only slightly above the general height of the plateau whose shore end was now occupied by General Canrobert's men.

Eager to make use of his opportunity, Lord Raglan cast many an anxious look down the track for G Battery. On getting his orders, Captain Turner had set off at once for the ford; but on reaching it, the lead horses refused to enter the water. Captain Lysons of the 23rd, who was taking a message back to General Evans, saw their trouble, and being on a steady old hunter, turned back and gave the guns a lead over the river. The first teams had hardly reached the other side, however, when a wheel horse was shot; and to add to the trouble a howitzer in the rear upset while going down the bank towards the river. This delayed most of the battery; but Captain Turner pressed on up the track with two guns. In their rapid advance the guns and mounted officers outstripped the detachments, and when they dropped into action they were short-handed. The artillery commander of the army, General Strangeways, was with Lord Raglan on the hill. He at once directed Colonel Collingwood Dickson and another officer to dismount and help man the guns. This they did most skilfully until the arrival of the gunners. The Causeway batteries on the main road formed the first target. The second shot found its mark; a limber was struck and two horses killed. The Russians, finding the Causeway guns were being taken in flank as well as being battered in front from de Lacy Evans' artillery, immediately withdrew them to a position higher up the road towards Sebastopol, where they produced small effect. The Russian reserves massed on the slopes of Kourgané Hill were dealt with next, and the dense columns provided an easy target. The range was quickly found, and round shot was seen to plough through the solid mass, causing the Russians to withdraw. This was about the time when the 1st Division was moving up to support the Light Division, for Lord Raglan was reported as calling out, 'Look how well the Guards and Highlanders advance.'

The two leading British divisions, covered by skirmishers, had moved steadily through the gardens and vineyards bordering the river, and had waded across. They found a momentary shelter in broken ground on the far side behind the bank bordering the slope up Kourgané Hill, but then their ordeal began. Clambering up over the bank behind their officers, they found they had to advance up a smooth hillside under heavy infantry and artillery fire. Soon gaps were torn in the thin red line, and it was a ragged, straggling and irregular formation which drew up towards the massed Russian columns. However, they were sufficiently linear to produce a continuous line of fire, with advantages over the restricted fire-power of the columns; and this was enough to bring success. The Russians could be seen opening out and trying to deploy; but too late; the British were close upon them. The Russian masses began to shake; the men in the rear were seen to run; then whole columns would turn and retire, halting and facing about at intervals. With Captain Turner's guns smashing their flank from Lord Raglan's mountain viewpoint, and with Codrington's and Pennefather's brigades of the Light Division still streaming upwards, the Russian troops could no longer hold their ground. They fled disordered up the hill.

The converging fire from the Russian batteries made a fearful havoc in the English ranks, and a wide street of dead and wounded stretching the whole way from the river upwards showed the nature of the fight. However, breathless, decimated and much broken, but with victory crowning their efforts, the centre regiments dashed right into the Great Redoubt and even captured two big guns which the Russian teams could not manage in time to hook in and drive away.

Soon after the capture of the Great Redoubt, however, Russian reserves moved down, and Codrington's brigade which had done so well, but whose effort was by now expended, was forced to give way before them. Victory for a moment seemed doubtful. The Guards were now coming up the hill; but some of Codrington's men rushing back down the slope from the Great Redoubt ran

56

into the centre of the second line, and forced it back too. When the Guards were able to move forward again, there was a huge hole in the middle of their ranks. Gradually, however, the torn lines moved on again, firing as they came, and once more the Russians drew back.

As the attack was made in échelon, the Highland Brigade, on the left of the Guards, were the last to enter the fight for Kourgané Hill; but after a spell of being galled by artillery fire short of the river, they were at last given the order to advance. There was difficulty in keeping in line as they passed the vineyards and orchards, for the men stumbled among the shallow pits in which the vines were planted; and had to open out as they made their way amongst the trees; and they got mixed up, and into a little confusion, wading through the river. The 42nd were the first across, and, dressing their line as they reached the far bank, moved straight up the hill. Next came the 93rd. Captain Ewart described their part in the battle. At the spot where his company crossed, the water was deep and came up to his breast. However, he was soon over, and giving his kilt a shake, got his men rapidly reformed. The regiment then advanced as before in line; but the Russians had got their eyes upon them; and at once opened fire, the guns from the Little Redoubt on the Russian right crossing with musketry fire from the front. One shell knocked over three or four of the light company under Captain Gordon, which was next to Ewart's; but on they rapidly went to the front. There was a Sousdal rifle regiment opposite the 93rd, and they shot Ensign Abercrombie through the heart, a sergeant through the body, and a corporal, a fine young lad, in the stomach. The whistling of the balls was something wonderful. One broke Ewart's scabbard, and Major MacGowan on the right got a ball through his kilt. Had they paused, they would have suffered a heavy loss; but nothing could exceed the impetuosity of the 93rd, opening fire by files as they advanced. The Russians were in column, and on getting nearer, the first Russian company brought down their bayonets as if to charge; but on the 93rd giving a cheer, they faced about and retired. Just as Captain Ewart was encouraging his men to follow them, waving his claymore over his head, up galloped Sir Colin. 'Halt, 93rd! Halt!' he shouted in his loudest tones, and they were all at once stopped in their career. It was perhaps as well, for the whole of the Russian cavalry were not far away on their left. Ewart had noticed them directly the 93rd had started mounting the slope, and had looked for the British cavalry; but they were not over the river. Lord Raglan had sent a

58   *Alma. 'Forward Forty Second!'*

59

staff officer with an order for the cavalry to cross by the bridge, but Lord Cardigan had started crossing at a ford, which caused some delay. As many of the 93rd had been knocked over by the time Ewart first saw the Russian Hussars and Cossacks, and as many others were blown, the regiment was in poor shape to receive cavalry; but nevertheless he called out to his men to be ready to form a company square if he gave the word, and kept an eye on the enemy horsemen. No charge, however, was made on them; and presently the whole of the Russian cavalry moved off. At this moment Lord Cardigan rode up, and Ewart saw him turn round and look anxiously behind for his brigade. As soon as it had crossed the Alma, he followed the Russians; but it was too late. At Simpheropol in 1856, after peace had been made, Ewart fell in with a Russian Hussar officer who told him he had been with his regiment at Alma. When asked why the Russian cavalry had not charged the Highlanders, he replied that they would have done so, but an A.D.C. from Prince Mentschikoff, who they quite thought was bringing them the order, had brought instructions for the cavalry to retreat.

On going back up the slope, the enemy, who had now withdrawn for the second time from the Great Redoubt, formed two large masses, and advanced to meet the 42nd. The 42nd were too blown to charge them, so they opened fire while advancing in line – an operation in which they had been well practised. In this way, amid cheers, they drove off in confusion the two original masses and further fugitives from the Redoubt.

Before reaching the inner crest of the heights, another body of troops came forward against the 42nd, and these were dealt with in the same way. Sir Colin had halted the 42nd on the inner crest of the heights, still firing and killing more of the enemy, when two more large columns came across from the direction of the Little Redoubt against their left flank. Just at this moment the 93rd appeared coming up from the river, and attacked these Russians. The 93rd, who were with difficulty withstrained from charging, had only time to fire and kill a few of these when bodies of fresh infantry came boldly against their left flank. But just at this moment the 79th in their turn came up from the river. The 79th went at these last troops cheering, and advancing while firing. They caused them great loss and forced them away in confusion. The whole operation was thus a most well conducted affair, and the échelon method of attack had proved very effective. While the Highland Brigade was advancing, the Guards on the right stormed and captured the Great Redoubt, and the Duke of Cambridge was able to ride his horse over the parapet, alongside the Coldstream.

Captain Hodasevich, with the Taroutine Regiment on Telegraph Hill, saw the advance of the 1st Division. He had never seen troops coming forward in line before, nor had he believed men could be found staunch enough to attack Russian massed columns in such a formation. He watched the thin red lines cross the river and approach the Great Redoubt; he saw them attack the Sousdal, Kazan and Auglitz regiments. He also saw the French coming up from the direction of the shore. They had left their own knapsacks on the other side of the river, and would have to go back for them after the battle; but now Russian knapsacks were to put them at a

A Piper of the 42nd Highlanders (Black Watch)

61

disadvantage. The Taroutine battalion purposely left their knapsacks on the ground when they retired; and the supporting Russian artillery trained their guns on them, waiting, and ready. Sure enough, the French mistook the knapsacks for men lying down, and first fired at them, and then charged them with the bayonet. Then the guns opened up, and the French suffered severely.

Hodasevich thought the battle went badly for the Russians because Prince Mentschikoff had too much confidence in his generals, taking them at their own estimation, having heard them boasting of past exploits. For example, General Kiriakoff, commanding the shore flank, told the Prince that his brigade alone was a match for any two allied divisions. What he had achieved in the Polish campaign was proof of that. Kvetzintzky and Gortschakoff on Telegraph Hill and Kourgané Hill also assured him that they could hold the strong Alma position for at least a week.

When the Russians started to give way, Prince Mentschikoff's limitations as a commander became obvious. He showed personal bravery, for when four of his staff were killed near him by fire from allied ships he remained unmoved. However, as Hodasevich said, courage is not the only quality required of a commander-in-chief. When it came to bringing up reserves to turn the British out of the Great Redoubt, he appeared impotent.

As the Russians began to retreat Prince Mentschikoff rode past Hodasevich's battalion which was clambering to the rear in disorder, and called out that it was a disgrace for a Russian soldier to retreat. An officer answered that if they had been ordered to stand their ground, they would have done so. But neither that officer nor anyone else understood that they were being ordered to stand there and then. The disorderly retreat just continued as before.

When the Russian retirement appeared widespread, Lord Raglan and his staff left their knoll beside the main road and trotted across towards the Great Redoubt to join the Duke of Cambridge. Afterwards they sought out Sir Colin Campbell. When the old Scot met him, Lord Raglan's eyes, Sir Colin noticed, began to fill 'and his lips and countenance to quiver'. He gave Sir Colin a cordial handshake in congratulation, but could not speak for emotion. The men cheered, and Sir Colin then said he was going to ask a favour. Could he have the honour of wearing the Highland bonnet during the rest of the campaign? The men cheered louder still; and Lord Raglan smiled and nodded his willing assent.

Lord Raglan now noticed that Lord Lucan had brought up C

and I Troops R.H.A. alongside the Highland Brigade, and that the guns were already in action against the retreating Russians. Lord Lucan, indeed, was impatiently awaiting orders for the cavalry to pursue; but Lord Raglan, anxious in his own phrase to keep his small cavalry force 'in a bandbox' for future tasks, gave orders for them to escort the guns a short distance forward only; and told Lord Lucan not to attack. When, in spite of this, the cavalry started galloping after some stragglers, Lord Raglan restrained them. He sent an A.D.C. forward to call them back to escort duty.

On the shore flank General Kiriakoff was also by this time withdrawing under fire from French guns moved up at last into position on the coastal plateau. For a time the Russians stood their ground on Telegraph Hill; but the eight depleted battalions there were no match for the whole French army. As Kiriakoff's men joined in the general Russian withdrawal, the Zouaves led the way to the summit of Telegraph Hill, ruthlessly bayoneting

Prince Mentschikoff

the few Russians left as rearguard. Then they hoisted the tricolour on the unfinished semaphore telegraph pillar, and stood cheering around it as if they had won the great victory of the Alma on their own. They convinced Marshal St. Arnaud. When he rode up to congratulate them, he fully believed that his troops had won the battle almost unaided; and this was the version transmitted to Paris in his despatch. Only his death a few days later prevented a serious quarrel developing between the allies, for the dissemination of such a false description of the battle greatly offended the British.

As far as Marshal St. Arnaud was concerned it was the end. He had been in the saddle since early morning and now it was half-past four. The excitement of the day had filled his dying body with a nervous energy, but now all was spent, and he rode away to take a rest. An orderly caught up with him bearing a message from Lord Raglan. It asked the French to join with the British in the pursuit. Marshal St. Arnaud replied that it was quite impossible. The knapsacks of the French army had been left on the other side

Surgeon Munro

of the river, and they would have to go back for them. Lord Raglan had wanted to pursue with his uncommitted 3rd Division; but he did not feel justified in doing so without the French, so orders were given to bivouac for the night on the ground where the army stood.

Before the Highland Brigade went into action Dr. Gibson had told Surgeon Munro to form his field hospital well back on the north side of the river; but thinking this too far in the rear, Munro had followed the 93rd down to the vineyards, in which he noticed several dead men of the 88th. As the 93rd went through the fields beside the river they suffered their first casualties; one man was killed and another badly wounded in the chest. Being close to a farmhouse, Munro took possession; and leaving the wounded man in charge of his orderly, continued with his three assistant surgeons to follow the regiment, dressing the wounded as they fell, and after applying field-dressings, sending them back to the farmhouse to which he later returned with one assistant after giving

Embarkation of the wounded

orders to the other two to stay with the regiment, one with each wing.

The farmhouse was a large one, and although the windows and doors were all completely smashed, and the walls loopholed in many places – for it had been occupied by the enemy – the floors and roof were uninjured; and in the yard were several stacks of straw, and a heap of firewood, so that Surgeon Munro soon had all the wounded, forty in number, on comfortable beds of straw, a couple of fires blazing, and arrangements made for the different operations that were necessary, and which should have been performed forthwith; except that he had received orders from the principal medical officers of the division and brigade, Doctors Gibson and Linton, not to perform any major operation until they were able to be present.

The doctors had also advised against the use of chloroform during operations. The day before the Alma a circular letter was issued by Dr. Hall, the principal medical officer of the army, cautioning regimental surgeons against its use, the caution almost amounting to a prohibition – at least no surgeon could have been blamed if, with the circular before him, he had declined to use chloroform. Surgeon Munro considered that this was a mistake, and an unnecessary interference with the regimental surgeons, who were, or should have been, men of experience, responsible for their acts, and for the treatment and management of their wounded. Indeed, he thought it was unwise to issue any instructions which might have been accepted as a prohibition of the use of an anaesthetic which would alleviate the suffering of a wounded soldier who was to undergo amputation of a shattered limb, even though a little danger might attend its administration. He did not know if many regimental surgeons were influenced by the circular, or deterred by it from using chloroform. Certainly he was not, for he administered it in every operation afterwards and without any ill effect.

At the farmhouse Surgeon Munro had a long wait for his superiors. They did not appear until after sunset, and consequently he had to tackle several operations by candlelight. They watched him perform a Syme's amputation at the ankle-joint, which was the first time it had ever been done in the field. No doubt duly impressed, Doctors Gibson and Linton then left, telling him to act in future on his own judgement and not await their approval. Munro said the ankle operation was a great success. When the Queen visited the Crimean wounded at Chatham later, she was very interested in the man concerned and asked about the wound and the operation – but not, Munro regretted, who had performed it! By midnight he had done all the operations required, seen all the wounds dressed and the men fed. Then, weary with the excitement and labour of the long day, he lay down to rest himself.

On the night of the battle the army bivouacked where it had stopped fighting, many of the regiments surrounded by their own dead and wounded comrades. The 93rd were fortunate in their bivouac, for the ground was comparatively clear and clean, and none of their dead or wounded was near them: the former had already been buried, and the wounded, numbering about a hundred, removed and comfortably provided for in Surgeon Munro's farmhouse down by the river. There were Russian dead lying about in front and rear, but these did not disturb as much as the presence of their own would have done.

The ground after the battle presented an appalling spectacle. There was wreck and ruin on every side: rifles, equipment, head-gear, clothing were scattered all about; in some places, dead men killed by bullets lay singly or in twos and threes near each other; in other places, those torn and mangled by shot and shell were piled in heaps; some who died in pain and agony had their eyes wide open and teeth firmly clenched with lips drawn tightly over them; and nearby, stretched upon his back with a placid expression on his pale face, eyes closed as if in sleep, rested one whose death had been instantaneous and painless. The whole night was spent by some surgeons seeking and attending to the wounded of their regiments; but in the 93rd, as the casualties were less numerous, the bandsmen by working hard and fearlessly had been able to remove all the dead and wounded while the fighting was going on, although three were wounded doing so.

The next days were spent burying the dead and removing the wounded and sick. On the afternoon of the second day the Duke of Cambridge visited Surgeon Munro's hospital. Having been told the necessary requirements to remove the wounded, the royal general sent up a few hours later a string of mules with litters and cacolets led by soldiers from the French ambulance corps. It took half an hour to load the wounded, and then they were taken away to be embarked onboard ship.

With the removal of the wounded the Battle of the Alma was over. The allied armies were now ready to move towards the next river, the Katcha, and then on to the Belbec and Sebastopol.

THE FLANK MARCH

THE FLANK MARCH

*'An attack on the South Side is not expected and will
give us the benefit of surprise.'*

GENERAL BURGOYNE

On 23 September, the allies marched forward again. Moving over
ground littered with enemy arms and accoutrements, they descended into the valley of the Katcha. The 93rd bivouacked in
orchards and vineyards around an attractive village which had
pleasant cottages with trellis porches. Emptied chests and broken
furniture showed the traces of Cossack spoilers, but the inhabitants had fled. At the Katcha, reinforcements disembarked on the
beaches for both armies, the 57th and Scots Greys joining the
British. As the latter rode in, the Highlanders turned out to cheer,
and Captain Ewart noticed that Sir Colin Campbell was wearing a
feather bonnet instead of a cocked hat. On getting Lord Raglan's
permission to wear a Highland bonnet after Alma, he found there
were plenty to spare, and as the 42nd wore red hackles, and the
79th and 93rd wore white, he had a hackle made partly red and
partly white.

Before leaving the Katcha, and moving towards the Belbec,
Lord Raglan ordered Lord Lucan with the bulk of the cavalry and
I Troop R.H.A. under Captain Maude to push forward on the left
flank and take possession of the village of Duvankoi on the upper
Belbec. Although watched by Cossacks while passing up a long
defile to the village, the English cavalry were not opposed; and
finding the place unoccupied, Lord Lucan took possession, even
though it was surrounded by hills and a death-trap. Lord Lucan
relied for defence on three guns on the road at the east end of the
village and three more at the west end, with some scouts on the
hills around. Having occupied the village for several hours, he
felt he had carried out his instructions, and withdrew all his
troops to the high ground above the village; but for a time, due to
Lord Lucan's rigid compliance with instructions, the cavalry were
in peril; and the incident was an earnest of what was to happen
later. In any case, the cavalry did not make a very successful

71

reconnaissance of the neighbourhood. Although they reported bodies of Russian troops near Sebastopol and Mackenzie's Farm,[1] they never discovered Prince Mentschikoff's headquarters only two miles away across the Belbec at Otarkoi.

Except for the cavalry the whole army bivouacked that night on the Katcha and on the next day marched a further seven miles to the Belbec. Lord George and the 4th Light Dragoons were still rearguard having been allotted the task because they were the last cavalry regiment out from home. The newly arrived Scots Greys, however, had gone straight up to the front; and the officers of the 4th Light Dragoons were peeved about it, and asked Lord George to see Lord Raglan. Lord Raglan was genial, but told the 4th Light Dragoons to stay where they were. He gave no reasons, but it was said later that he wanted to make sure that the Russians realized that the allies had received strong reinforcements. The sight of a lot of new grey horses might do this.

The 4th Division, and the 4th Light Dragoons, were a day's march in the rear, and quite detached from the rest of the army; General Cathcart was worried about his security, and sent an A.D.C. escorted by two troopers of the 4th Light Dragoons to explain to Lord Raglan his unsafe position. Losing the way in the dark, the A.D.C. got too close to the North Side of Sebastopol, and his party was shot at by a Russian outpost. One of the orderlies was killed, as well as the horse of the other; so the live man jumped on the live horse and followed the A.D.C. Because of this the 4th Light Dragoons were able to claim they had the first man killed by fire from Sebastopol. Half an hour after this party had gone, Lord George was called upon to find further escorts. This time it was for another of General Cathcart's staff to take on an important message to Admiral Lyons of the inshore squadron. The message had originated from Lord Raglan, and was to be transmitted to Admiral Dundas in command of the fleet. It told the navy to proceed to Balaclava.

This decision to move round to the south of Sebastopol was arrived at because of the reluctance of the French to attack from the north. After Alma Marshal St. Arnaud refused to pursue because his men had to return back across the river for their knapsacks. He was also impressed by General Kiriakoff's rearguard a few miles back on the road to Sebastopol. These Russians

1. *There were a number of Scots in Russia; for example a General Read commanded the main attack on the French and Sardinians at Tractir Bridge.*
The end-paper map illustrates this chapter.

looked all the more formidable because they concealed the rabble behind them. Later St. Arnaud said that the French were unable to advance and assault the North Side because his men were tired. Lord Raglan could not believe this, and sought to try to persuade him to change his mind, but the marshal now had still further objections to pushing on. While the allied armies remained halted on the Katcha, the French reported a new emplaced battery commanding the mouth of the Belbec; and Marshal St. Arnaud said that as the French would move forward opposite the new-formed battery they should be the judge of whether the advance on Sebastopol should continue. Moreover, the enemy had sunk men-of-war across the mouth of the Sebastopol roadstead, and thus little help could be had from the fleet. He asked that the march might be postponed until ten o'clock to give him time to reconnoitre the new field-work and consider the impact of the sinkings. This request was brought by General Trochu with the additional information that five warships and two frigates had been sunk in the entrance to the harbour and that the new work in advance of the main Star Fort commanded the beach by the mouth of the Belbec where siege materials and supplies were planned to be disembarked.

Lord Raglan had of course to agree to the delay; but he did manage to persuade the French to move forward a little way at ten o'clock without committing themselves to an attack. Thus, not long afterwards, the leaders mounted the hills by the Belbec and looked down upon Sebastopol with its white buildings and green copper onion-shaped domes shining in the sun. A long deep stretch of blue water, on which many ships were riding at anchor, cut the town in two. The South Side was again divided by Man-of-War Harbour along which could be seen dockyard installations, arsenals and barracks on the left bank, and the churches and the main buildings of the town on the right. There appeared to be few fortifications guarding the South Side, but facing them on the North Side was the huge Star Fort. This work had been built in 1818 to guard Fort Constantine on the north entrance of the roadstead from attack in reverse by marines landing on the west coast; but it also stood in the path of invaders from the Belbec, and could be used against the allies. It was an octagon with sides about 200 yards long, mounting forty-seven guns, twelve facing the north. For a week 1,500 labourers had been working day and night on additional works on either flank. Two batteries in a crescent were set up on the north-west against shipping, with two guns covering the mouth of the Belbec. It was the earthwork

Plan of Sebastopol

prepared for these two guns which had scared Marshal St. Arnaud. Altogether by 25 September there were twenty-nine guns in battery facing the allies as well as Russian ships placed in position in the roadstead to sweep with broadsides its slopes on the North Side. It was learnt later that only 11,000, mostly sailors, defended the North Side; but that they were commanded by Admiral Korniloff, a deeply religious and stirringly patriotic man, who ordered the priests to bless the defenders and their defences, and declared, 'If I give the order to retreat, kill me with your bayonets.'

Opinions differ as to whether the allies should have attacked the North Side. Kinglake, agreeing with Colonel Todleben, the defender of Sebastopol, believed it would have brought them certain success. Hamley, on the other hand, considered Todleben so inaccurate that his views were suspect. Hamley thought that once the Russians had blocked the entrance to the harbour so that

74

the allied navy could not give fire support, an attack on the North Side would have failed. The Russian ships and the guns of Star Fort and its extensions would, he believed, have brought 'an exterminating fire to bear'.

Lord Raglan and Admiral Lyons were at first anxious to attack the North Side, and the admiral was sent to try to persuade the French to co-operate. Upon hearing of the marshal's fear of the new field-work, Admiral Lyons ran in close on board a small steamer and found no guns yet emplaced. He reported this to the French commander, but could not persuade him to change his mind.

The whole operation now seemed ruined, and in despair Lord Raglan considered again the idea of a southern attack on Sebastopol. Mr. Oliphant, a Scottish traveller who had studied the land defences of Sebastopol, had written in his book published in 1853 that however well fortified might be the approaches to Sebastopol, there was nothing whatever to prevent any number of troops landing a few miles south of the town in one of the convenient bays like Kamiesh, Kazatch and Balaclava and marching into it. Provided they were strong enough to defeat any military force that might be opposed to them in the open field, they could easily sack the town and burn the fleet. Moreover, 'there was fair ground for believing that no new defences had been set up recently'. Before he left England Lord Raglan saw Mr. Oliphant, and on leaving Bulgaria planned at first to land on the south coast as Oliphant suggested. Thus he now conceived the idea of trying to persuade the French to join with him in marching across country to the south coast, and there setting up bases from which to attack Sebastopol's South Side.

Although it was an extremely risky affair to march right round the town where the Russian army was concentrated and offer a long line of advance to be taken in flank, nevertheless the enemy, having already been beaten, might well be too cowed to make use of their opportunity. Also the Flank March, as it came to be called, was a way of getting moving again. The French had refused to attack the North Side. Short of abandoning the campaign altogether there appeared no other alternative. The march also conveniently spared the French from attacking, put the English in the lead for the first time, and gave them virtual control of the new operation.

Lord Raglan now consulted his general of engineers, John Burgoyne; and he found him enthusiastic for a southern approach from which to start the siege. Burgoyne, a wizened

General Burgoyne

seventy-two-year-old, had been present at the capture of Ciudad Rodrigo in 1812 and conducted the storming of the castle at San Sebastian as commanding engineer. He not only advanced cogent reasons for moving round to the south of Sebastopol, but he put the case so convincingly in person to Marshal St. Arnaud that the ailing French commander gave his provisional approval. Burgoyne's arguments followed closely those of Hamley. He said that the South Side had fewer permanent fortifications and these extended over a greater distance; that an attack on the south was not expected and would give the allies the benefit of surprise; that the North Side, even if taken, would not give control over the

South Side; and that there were good harbours in the south to land the siege-train.

Lord Raglan went over himself for the final conference with the French commander and found Marshal St. Arnaud sitting rigidly in a chair with his hands gripping the arm rests. Asked to confirm his earlier provisional acceptance of the new plan, he did no more than nod his head. As they left, one of Lord Raglan's staff commented on the French commander's strange behaviour; but Lord Raglan had understood why Marshal St. Arnaud had been so stiff and unfriendly. 'Didn't you realize it,' he answered, 'he is dying.' Not long afterwards, St. Arnaud was in the agonies of cholera, but by then the march around Sebastopol had begun, and with the English leading the way.

While the armies lay on the Belbec a detachment of cavalry under Lord Cardigan went forward and returned with valuable information about a marsh between the English and Sebastopol, so that, when the march began, the leaders at once bent to the left and were able to avoid a serious obstacle. Lord Raglan's plan was to move south-south-east over the wooded hills around Sebastopol and strike the main road out of the town at Mackenzie's Farm. It was to begin as a reconnaissance in force by the English. When the way was seen to be clear, the French would follow. Then the two armies would march on, one behind the other, down to the Tchernaya, cross the river at the Tractir Bridge, march over the North Valley of Balaclava, cross the famous Woronzoff Road and Causeway Heights, go over the South Valley of Balaclava, pass through the village of Kadikoi, and so to Balaclava. From Mackenzie's Farm to the Causeway Heights they were on the main route to Sebastopol; but from then on they left it, for it followed the Woronzoff Road back up on to the Chersonese Plateau to reach Sebastopol through a cutting by the Quarries near the Redan.

According to the maps there was a woodland road which led from the Belbec to Mackenzie's Farm; and Lord Raglan allotted this to the cavalry and artillery. The infantry were told to spread themselves and make their way through the woods on a compass bearing. Meanwhile, Lord Raglan rode off with a small escort to spy out the land and study the route ahead. Riding confidently through the woods he mounted the west shoulder of the knoll on which the lighthouse stood at the head of Sebastopol Roadstead. From here he was able to see that the way to Balaclava was clear of enemy. Turning, he looked back at Sebastopol and could make

77

out few defences except for the Malakoff and the Redan on the South Side. On the North Side was the great Star Fort, now left behind and avoided. Leaving the lighthouse, Lord Raglan led his party back through the woods to rejoin his army. With an unerring eye for country he made his way up and down the hills and through the trees towards the woodland road the cavalry were following.

Meanwhile the infantry had been proceeding through the woods with great difficulty, directed by compass. Captain Adye overheard the Duke of Cambridge remarking, 'I have received many orders in my day; but this is the first time I have ever marched by compass.' It was a harassing march. Munro relates how the 93rd toiled up-hill through forest and dense undergrowth along narrow tracks 'in many places scarcely discernible'. The regimental officers had no knowledge where they were going. They had heard about the Star Fort and the new defence works which scared Marshal St. Arnaud and they fully expected at any moment, and at every temporary halt, to get orders to attack them. They had no idea they were moving in another direction. During the march the men suffered terribly from thirst due to the effort of pushing through the brushwood in overpowering heat – for not a breath of air penetrated the dense woodland. Munro, however, heard no complaints from the 93rd. The only interruption was when a man fell down in the agonies of cholera crying out painfully and faintly for the water they were unable to give him because their little barrels were empty. They carried the poor man along with them on a stretcher for a time; and found it very difficult to get through the undergrowth. When the man died they laid him in a hastily dug grave by the side of the track. This was the first case of cholera in the 93rd, and they did not have another until just before the battle of Balaclava.

From an instinctive knowledge of country without even checking from his map, Lord Raglan, as if he had known the country all his life, soon struck the woodland road bending up towards Mackenzie's Farm, which he had allotted to the cavalry and artillery. Lord Lucan had moved along this road guided by Major Wetherall of the Q.M.'s department; but on coming to a fork, had allowed his guide to lead him the wrong way along a mere track which soon came to nothing. When the artillery reached the fork, they halted, wondering what to do. A stray trooper pointed out the way Lord Lucan had gone; but Captain Maude, whose Troop was leading, said it was a 'mere woodcutting road' and he could not take his guns along it. Fortunately at this juncture Lord Raglan rode up, and, having been told what had happened, took the lead, telling the artillery to follow him. After about a mile, just before Mackenzie's Farm, they reached a point in the lane where the light was showing through the trees in such a way as to suggest they were near the edge of the forest, and General Airey, Raglan's Chief of Staff, went ahead to investigate. He galloped off up the road to the opening, and then suddenly reined up and raised his hand as if to signal the whole column to halt and keep very quiet. Just in time he had stopped his horse from taking him out of the wood on to the main road from Sebastopol. On the road, strolling about, smoking, and leaning against the sides of wagons which stretched in a long line down the hill to the north, were groups of Russian soldiers. They were obviously the rearguard of a large force resting on the march. And the wagons, Airey noticed with surprise, were facing away from Sebastopol.

It so happened that Prince Mentschikoff, ignorant of the allies' change of plan, was moving a considerable force inland from Sebastopol to take them in the flank; and as Lord Raglan and his staff had emerged from the woods on to the open ground about Mackenzie's Farm, they had stumbled on his rearguard. In fact, both the opposing forces were making a flank march using the same road.

Lord Raglan took charge at once. Cool and composed, he quietly sent off two officers to bring up the cavalry. Then he moved forward slowly and peered through the foliage at the surprised Russians who could not understand what was happening. After standing as if stupefied for a moment, they finally decided they were likely to be set upon by the men in blue half-hidden among the trees; and jumping on their wagons, drove hurriedly away towards the north.

Lord Lucan was one of the first to appear. Lord Raglan remarked icily as he rode past, 'Lord Lucan, you're late.' But he galloped on without answering. The cavalry continued to come up; and by this time Captain Maude's I Troop had emerged from the woods and dropped into action in the clear space around the farm. Covering the road, the guns opened fire on the enemy wagons disappearing in the distance. B Troop were the next into action, and then the field batteries. Soon all were adding their contribution. To cover the flank of his main body, Lord Raglan dismounted some of the Greys and sent them to man the wood on the north side of the road, and then with his staff and the rest of the cavalry rode forward boldly against a rearguard of about twenty Russian infantrymen who faced about and delivered a volley in their faces. But the Russians fired high, and then being overridden, either scattered into the woods or were sabred as they stood, and when the cavalry reached the crest from which the road goes steeply down into the plain beyond, Lord Raglan called off the pursuit.

A large number of wagons were captured and a few prisoners taken including an officer. There was plenty of booty to choose from in the overturned carts, and the troopers seized hold of sheepskin coats, hussars' fur-lined pélisses and bottles of coarse brandy. The officer prisoner was found to be dead-drunk. When Lord Raglan tried to interrogate him, he merely reeled from side to side proffering eternal friendship. Lord Raglan, upset at seeing an officer in this state, sent him away in disgust. When Lord Cardigan appeared, Lord Raglan turned on him sharply, saying, 'The cavalry were out of their proper place. You took them much too low down.' But Lord Cardigan excused himself. 'My Lord, I am no longer in command of the cavalry,' he exclaimed primly.

This was not quite the end of the affair at Mackenzie's Farm. Two days later when the 4th Division were resting in the neighbourhood in the rear of the allied army, General Cathcart told Lord George he had a little job for him, which might have a good effect, and which at all events would be good fun. He had just seen Prince Napoleon whose division had gone on towards Balaclava, and was told that the road by which the Russians had retreated to the north was still covered with their débris, including ammunition wagons. Cathcart asked him to follow up the line of their retreat and blow up some of these wagons. He gave him a limit of three miles and two hours.

Well pleased with his assignment, Lord George set off down the main road northwards with a picked detachment on the regiment's freshest horses, and two engineers. What a scene met their eyes! Every description of accoutrement and engine of warfare, with an occasional wagon upset, and here and there a dead horse or two, strewed the road which wound through the woods. The English gunners had done their work well!

After going the allotted three miles, Lord George came upon a hill down which the road descended by zigzag turns to the plains towards Bakschi Serai and Simpheropol. He halted his party, and had hardly done so, before they were fired at by a group of half-a-dozen Cossacks, and heard the ping-ping of bullets whistling over their heads. But the Cossacks did not linger to correct their aim. Mounting, they made off at full gallop down the steep winding road to rejoin their main body. The road down the hill, with its many turns, was even more cluttered than the previous section had been, and offered just the opportunity they sought. Quickly the engineers dismounted and set their charges. The slow matches lit, they all scuttled away, but not before one wagon had blown up prematurely and nearly taken their heads off. Their allotted time had now been nearly used up, and they returned to Mackenzie's Farm as fast as they could. Before they reached it the wagons started blowing up one after another, sounding to the rest of the division very much like a general action. They thought Lord George's detachment must have been caught in a trap. They sprang to arms and dashed off down the road to help Lord George's men. General Cathcart and his staff were the first to arrive, galloping at top speed and looking much alarmed. On meeting them he said, 'Thank God you are safe! I was afraid I had got you into a mess.' Lord George then explained how lucky he had been to find the mass of wagons stuck on the hill, and received warm thanks for his efforts.

The army moved on again, and in a short time Lord Raglan was leading it down from the heights east of Sebastopol by a steep winding mountain road into the valley of the Tchernaya towards the Tractir Bridge. It was nearly dark before the bulk of the British troops reached the river, and some did not arrive that night. The 93rd crossed over and bivouacked on the top of a hill which they could not afterwards identify, but believed was one of the Fedioukine hills. So tired and exhausted were the men that they threw themselves on the ground and refused to eat or drink, even to take their rum, an example of self-denial unusual amongst soldiers, no matter how tired or exhausted. Munro had accompanied the 93rd on many a march, but had never seen the men so completely done up as they were at the end of the famous Flank March round Sebastopol.

Next morning the allied advance was resumed. First they crossed the North Valley of Balaclava; then they went over the Causeway Heights and Woronzoff Road and approached the port across South Valley towards the pleasant little village of Kadikoi. Beyond Kadikoi a bend in the road brought them to the edge of what seemed to be a small inland pool with a rivulet trickling into it, with the rest of the sheet of water hidden behind the fold of the hill. Beyond the pool, but still very close at hand, there rose a barrier of towering hills, and one of them was crowned with an antique castle in ruins.

According to Captain Adye, as the staff and leading troops approached, a deputation of the inhabitants of Balaclava came forward bearing bread and salt as a token of submission. Almost at the same time a gun was fired from the old castle on the heights; and a shot splashed in the water close by, followed by another. Lord Raglan through an interpreter asked the reason for this unexpected demonstration, as bread and salt and bursting shells seemed inconsistent with each other; but the only explanation they could give was that the small garrison had not been summoned to surrender. Some of the leading Light Division were then sent swarming up the flanking heights of the pool; and half C Troop R.H.A. under Captain Brandling dropped into action, while the other half under Captain Adye went up the steep hill overlooking the castle to find a better position from which to bombard it. By hooking detachment horses with web breast-harness in front of the ordinary teams the ascent was successfully made, and the gunners, and the 77th who accompanied them, were able from the new position to look right into the fort. Then, just as the guns got into action, there roared out a thunder of other guns from behind the castle. All knew what it was. The navy had arrived.

Finding themselves under a converging fire from three sides, the small garrison of local militia hoisted a white handkerchief on a pole in token of surrender. The commandant, an old Greek colonel named Monto, had been wounded in the foot, and was carried down to Balaclava where he was met by Lord Raglan and his staff who had just ridden in. Asked why he had taken upon himself to open fire without having means to attempt a real defence, Colonel Monto answered that he had never been summoned to surrender. He said that if he had been, he would have done so at once; but he thought that, until he should be either attacked or summoned to surrender, it was his duty to offer resistance – later, Colonel Monto became something of a Russian national hero for this show of resistance. His wife, on seeing her husband's condition, rushed out of her house by the waterfront in a flood of tears, fell on his neck and kissed him repeatedly. Lord Raglan, however, spoke kindly and reassured her. In the meantime some Russian ladies who had left Sebastopol and taken refuge in Balaclava, terrified by the sudden arrival of the British, crossed the harbour in a small boat in a vain hope of escape. Accompanied by another officer Captain Adye followed them across and tried to reassure them. Knowing nothing of the language they found this difficult. They tried 'Buono, Russ buono',

82

but it was not sufficient. Fortunately they discovered that one of the ladies could understand a little French and were able to persuade them in that language to return to the village where they were taken care of. Many years later in 1872, on revisiting the Crimea with Gordon of Khartoum, Captain Adye found the old commandant was still alive, and they called on him. He was very pleased to see them and to talk over old days, and said that he would never forget the kindness he had received from the English when a prisoner. The officers and men of the navy in the man-of-war which took him to Constantinople treated him, he said, like a prince.

When Lord Raglan rode through the streets of Balaclava the inhabitants dropped to their knees in supplication, holding up loaves of bread in their outstretched hands. However, they took heart again when they saw how genial the English commander looked. Riding forward to the waterside, Lord Raglan scanned the basin before him. Shut in by steep lofty hills it looked like a tarn or small lake. The maps, however, showed that it was indeed the port of Balaclava; and as if to prove it, a small vessel came gliding in carrying the British flag. Once more the land and the sea forces had met. 'If Lyons were here,' Lord Raglan exclaimed, 'it would be perfect.' 'He is not far away,' he was told; and sure enough Admiral Lyons was close by in the *Agamemnon*, the vessel responsible for the shots at the castle.

From on board the vessel that had run in, soundings were quickly taken, and small as it was, the pool proved deep enough to float a ship of the line. Soon the harbour was crowded with shipping, and the town with British soldiery.

The next day when the first French divisions arrived, they questioned the British presence in an area which, facing north, was the right of the line. When the flank march was agreed on, it was said, Balaclava was to be used by the allies, not by one of them only. It had not then been realized that it was so small; but now with the basin crowded with ships and the landing-place and single street swarming with men, it was obvious that Balaclava was too diminutive to be divided. The French, however, had been assigned the right of the line, and unless their precedence was conceded, Balaclava, as the easternmost of all the possible landing-places on the south coast, must needs be theirs.

By this time General Canrobert had taken over the command of the French army, and he acted with great forbearance in the matter. Seeing the British already installed in the port and the town, and realizing that to call upon them to move out and make way for the French would be likely to create bad blood, he generously gave Lord Raglan the choice. The facilities of Kamiesch and Kazatch bays were then not known, so the opportunity of keeping Balaclava seemed to have great value. Before deciding, Lord Raglan asked Admiral Lyons' opinion, and on receiving his support he made the fatal decision of staying in Balaclava, with all its consequences. These were serious. It meant that being on the right, the British had to guard the allied flank as well as play their part in the siege.

THE FIRST BOMBARDMENT

✡

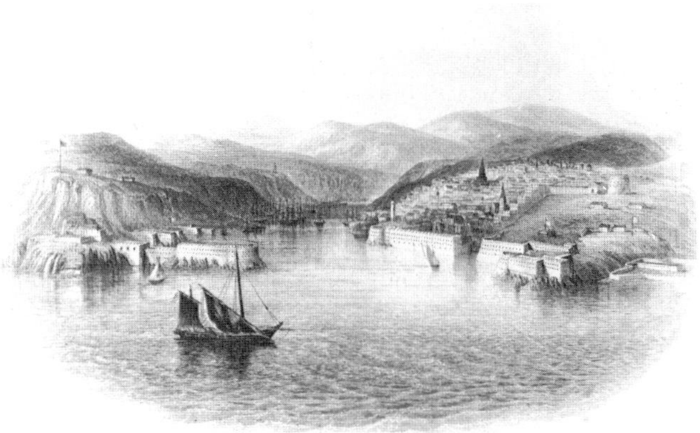

THE FIRST BOMBARDMENT

*'Some of the defenders were daring enough to rush
upon the shells as they fell, draw the fuse, and thus
prevent them bursting, and saving the lives of their
comrades. In the Russian forces anyone who did this
successfully was awarded the Cross of St. George.
This was much valued by the men as its award
exempted them from flogging.'*

HODASEVICH

Lord Raglan wanted to assault Sebastopol immediately; but the
French never liked attacking without full artillery support, and
on this occasion General Canrobert exclaimed that to do so would
be too rash to be even contemplated for one moment. 'It would be
utterly unjustifiable, almost a crime,' he said. 'Particularly
when our home governments have both supplied us with magnificent siege trains!'

General Burgoyne agreed with the French view about waiting
for the heavy guns; but not about their plan to assault the Russian
central defence works. Having surveyed the position with Lord
Raglan, he considered the great tower of the Malakoff on their
right was the key of the whole position; and that 'a good site or
sites for not less than eight guns should be sought for to demolish
that tower'. The French, however, demurred; and it was finally
decided that the main attack would be made by them on the
Flagstaff Bastion, the earthworks to their immediate front.
Captain Adye thought that, as at the end of the siege, which lasted
nearly a year, Sebastopol fell chiefly by an assault on the very
position originally indicated by General Burgoyne, it was a
striking proof of the clear insight and great ability of that distinguished soldier. General Cathcart was horrified at the allied
commanders' decision to wait to land the siege artillery before
making any attack. The 4th Division were at last in the front line;
and he was confident that if only given the order to advance, they
could walk straight into Sebastopol. 'Land the siege trains!' he
exclaimed. 'But my dear Lord Raglan, what the devil is there to
knock down?'

87

At this stage there was very little: on the east stood a round tower with four guns, the Malakoff, just north of Mamelon Hill; on the west was a crenellated wall with another tower, the Quarantine land bastion, overlooking Quarantine Bay; and between were two sets of earthworks as yet unfinished and un-armed, the Flagstaff Bastion and the Redan just north of the Quarries.

During the first fortnight of October the allied armies were occupied in landing and moving up heavy guns and ammunition from Kamiesch and Balaclava, and in constructing batteries and digging trenches in front of Sebastopol. It was arranged that the bombardment should open on 17 October, followed by an assault by the French whose works were closer to the Russian defences. Owing to the hard ground on the right which did not allow deep entrenchments, the British had their batteries farther back and could only give long-range support; but their infantry were expected to support the French assault. At the same time as the land bombardment the combined fleets were to attack the forts at the mouth of the harbour. Lord Raglan's order said that the fire upon Sebastopol would begin at 6.30 a.m. from the French and English batteries in co-operation with the allied fleets – the signal to be the discharge of three mortars by the French. The troops off duty were to be ready to fall in at a moment's notice; the horses of the field batteries were to be harnessed; and a thousand seamen with heavy guns were to be landed from the British fleet to form a naval brigade to act in conjunction with the Royal Artillery.

The navies in fact were of more use in the field than they were at sea, for the naval bombardment of the forts at the entrance of Sebastopol harbour was most disappointing. Matters were not helped by lack of liaison between the British and French navies; and the incompatibility of Admiral Dundas who commanded the British fleet and Admiral Lyons in command of the inshore squadron. Lord Raglan found Dundas obstructive, difficult and excessively cautious; but he and Lyons became close personal friends and this Dundas resented. Although undercurrents of hostility made the co-operation of the navy and the army difficult to arrange, at first all seemed to go well, for Admiral Dundas accepted Lord Raglan's commission to start to fire on the forts at the same time as the armies' land batteries began, and wrote, 'You may depend upon my using every exertion, with Admiral Hamelin my French colleague, to aid you in your object.'

On 17 October, however, everything went wrong; and particularly as regards the naval contribution. At half-past ten on the

88

Admiral Dundas

previous evening Admiral Dundas on board the *Britannia* received a message from Admiral Hamelin saying he would not open fire until 10.30 next morning as the shot would not last long and if used up too early the enemy would think they had been beaten off. Dundas rather unwillingly agreed to conform with the French as to the timing of the naval bombardment; but next morning Admiral Hamelin came aboard the *Britannia* and confronted Dundas with yet another change of plan. Following instructions from General Canrobert, his supreme commander, the French fleet proposed to deliver their fire on the forts in line at anchor, and at a distance. Even the cautious Dundas would not

89

agree to conform with this, so each navy adopted a different tactic, and neither succeeded. Although the French guns on their own outnumbered those ashore almost five to one, the forts were made of hard limestone from the Steppes, and the ships were nearly all of wood. Very few guns were disabled, and only fifty Russians were killed or wounded. The British fared even worse. At least the French ships were too far away to suffer much damage. The British captains, however, despite Dundas' signal to keep well out, decided a show of spirit must be made, and went in to attack the forts. Admiral Lyons' fine screw-ship *Agamemnon* in the lead

Admiral Lyons

was hit in several places; the *Sanspareil* and *London* received heavy damage; and the *Bellerophon* was set on fire. At half-past five, when Admiral Dundas gave the signal to haul off, 300 British sailors had been killed or wounded and enormous quantities of ammunition expended; but the forts were hardly damaged at all.

The bombardment from the allied land batteries was more successful, as Captain Ewart's account shows. After the flank march, Captain Ewart left the 93rd Sutherland Highlanders and became an intelligence officer at headquarters. As he put it, 'Stanton of the Engineers most good-naturedly lent me a spare blue frock-coat which he happened to have; a Russian hussar sabre was substituted for my claymore, and I was transformed into a Deputy-Assistant-Quartermaster-General, minus a cocked hat, but with the addition of 9s. 6d. a day to my pay.' On the night of 16 October, he was sent off to take final orders to the five generals of division: the Duke of Cambridge, Sir George de Lacy Evans, Sir Richard England, Sir George Cathcart and Sir George Brown. Then, at six o'clock next morning, he went with Lord Raglan and the headquarters staff to a hill in front of General England's 3rd Division and watched the whole operation.

The first gun was fired at twenty minutes to seven, and there began a terrific shower of shot and shell from all the allied batteries, while the Russians replied from the Malakoff, from the guns they had now emplaced in the Redan, and from the Flagstaff bastion opposite the French. It was a grand sight and the noise of the cannonade marvellous – to Ewart's ears at least!

At half-past seven he was sent off by General Airey the chief-of-staff to see how the British batteries were doing against the Malakoff. It was not a pleasant duty for he knew he would be exposed to fire from the Malakoff and from the east face of the Redan both when approaching and leaving the batteries. However, he put spurs to his horse and galloped off. Shot and shell were passing over the batteries and falling in the rear, and he felt this ride might well be his last. His Russian charger, captured near Mackenzie's Farm, seemed rather to enjoy it and carried him safely right into one of the batteries which was manned by sailors. The naval officer in command appeared wonderfully confident and said all was going well. On his return Ewart met the Duke of Cambridge not far from the battery.

About eleven o'clock, the main French magazine blew up at Mount Rodolph, the large work opposite Central and Flagstaff Bastions. Consequently the French guns ceased, many of them

91

having been dismounted, and the British had to try and double their fire to compensate for this misfortune to their allies. The combined fleets could now be heard bombarding the forts facing the sea. The roar of their cannon was tremendous; but the men-of-war soon became enveloped in smoke, and their masts could only occasionally be seen.

At two o'clock a shell from one of the British batteries caused the explosion of a large Russian magazine in the Redan. This was greeted with tremendous cheers from the British side. Soon afterwards a Russian shell set fire to several cases of gunpowder in the rear of Gordon's Battery, fortunately, however, doing no material damage. The fire from the Lancaster guns in battery on the extreme right was principally directed at a Russian three-decker in the harbour; but the vessel did not seem to be hit very often.

After the unfortunate explosion of the French magazine, a sortie was made by the Russians to spike the French guns at Mount Rodolph; but it was gallantly repulsed by a charge of the Chasseurs de Vincennes. This little incident was very exciting and the staff on the hill had a capital view of it.

General Burgoyne remained near Lord Raglan most of the day and Ewart's brother in the Royal Engineers was with him. Lord Raglan had a good meal sent up from his headquarters, and kindly invited all the staff to have lunch with him. During the day a bag of letters and newspapers was brought up, a mail-boat having arrived. While Ewart was standing near, Lord Raglan opened a packet of newspapers and drew out *The Times* of 3 October. The first thing that caught his eye were the words 'Fall of Sebastopol' in large letters, followed by a long account giving the number of ships taken and prisoners captured. Ewart glanced at his lordship's face and noticed the expression of annoyance which came over it as he put the paper down. Ewart was also angry about the bogus report. What he had been looking forward to reading about was the reception in England of the news of the victory on the Alma where the 93rd had done so well. He had, however, something else to do besides read newspapers, and turned away to watch the bombardment. The English fire, he noticed, 'was playing the mischief with the Russian defences'. In fact, had the French been able to give support, the Russians' fire might have been subdued sufficiently for an assault to be made. With the French *hors de combat*, however, the chance was lost, and when night fell the Russians set to work to repair their batteries, and the dismounted guns were replaced by others.

Captain Ewart was next sent to find out what the ground was like opposite the picquets of the 2nd Division. This was just beyond a spot named by the British, Shell Hill, from the number of these missiles which had fallen there. It was on the extreme right of the line near the Lancaster Battery in the area which later became the battlefield of Inkerman. Although occupied by Russian outposts, Ewart was told he must go, but could take a hussar orderly with him. Having buckled on his compass and mounted his horse, he started off followed by his hussar to whom on arriving at the 2nd Division camp he handed over his charger. Going forward on foot, he soon reached the British advanced sentries; and getting out pencil and paper crept on forward cautiously, 'feeling tolerably certain' that in a few minutes he would either have a bullet through him or be taken prisoner. In fact neither happened. But something less expected. He had not gone far when suddenly he heard a noise behind, and turning round, saw two companies of British soldiers doubling to the front in extended order with Colonel the Hon. Percy Herbert, A.Q.M.G. of the 2nd Division, riding at their head. This apparition soon attracted enemy fire, including round shot from a battery next to the lighthouse at the head of Sebastopol Roadstead; and the area becoming too hot for sketching, Ewart rode off back to present a verbal report.

Captain Hodasevich describes what it was like inside the walls of Sebastopol during the first bombardment. His company of the Taroutine Regiment divided its time between manning the wall joining the Central Bastion to the Flagstaff Bastion, and being in reserve in the Place du Théâtre. They were opposite Mount Rodolph on which were the main French batteries, so were in the forefront of the battle. He says that Colonel of Engineers Todleben visited all the bastions and batteries every day and watched constantly the allied trenches being pushed forward, and the changing position of their guns, so that he could make his own defences conform to his advantage. For example, when he noticed a salient developing in the French trenches opposite the Central Bastion, he first set up one of his own batteries to enfilade it, and then he had a part of the parapet of the Flagstaff Bastion thrown back to take six guns of large calibre to bring crossfire on the same place so that the trench was completely commanded. Whenever he noticed allied earthworks being pushed forward, he immediately made some change in his own to meet them. Sometimes this object was gained by simply changing the position of a gun, or by altering an embrasure to bear upon the point required. If this did not suffice, the whole battery was remade. Such were Todleben's tactics which won him his immortal fame! To some extent the fact that the South Side of Sebastopol was originally unfortified helped the Russians, for nearly all the defences there were erected to meet specific threats and could easily be adapted as circumstances changed.

Early in October the Taroutine Regiment was manning the ground in the ravine between the Central and Flagstaff Bastions with some of them at work on a reserve battery behind Flagstaff Bastion, and Hodasevich went up on to the roof of a house nearby and watched the cannonade. A red flag was hoisted on Flagstaff Bastion from where Admiral Korniloff was supervising the firing as a signal to the other batteries. Then they all hoisted red flags in acknowledgement, and a tremendous bombardment was opened from all sides. To Hodasevich the shooting appeared accurate, with the shells falling in the allied trenches and bursting very well; but afterwards when he joined the group of officers round the admiral, he found him pointing out the places where quite a

Sebastopol, from the Central Bastion

number of guns had been off target. The allies had stopped work on their saps and trenches while the Russian bombardment was in progress; but the moment it stopped, they started to work again vigorously. Hodasevich would see distinctly the earth being thrown out of the trenches on to the breastworks, and was astonished at the quantity thrown up at each shovelful, believing the allies must be using machines to dig with. Later they had an opportunity of examining English shovels, as a number were taken from the Turkish redoubts after the battle of Balaclava; and they were astonished how much better they were than their own. This, Hodasevich explained, was because of faulty Russian administration. All regimental tools in Russia were kept in store, to be shown when required, but not for use. They were painted annually, and the Russian colonels drew money for replacements when necessary; but usually they pocketed the money without checking for faulty ones. When they came to be used, they had never been tested, and many were good for nothing. In Hodasevich's company the men broke all their tools after three days' work, and were in consequence obliged to get new ones, which were little better.

When Hodasevich's men had finished their work on the battery behind Flagstaff Bastion, they were sent to relieve the second battalion behind the stone wall between Central and Flagstaff Bastions. They were then ordered to send out advanced sentries. Volunteers for this were first called for, but few offered themselves so the required number were detailed. As soon as it was dark, Captain Hodasevich with Ensign Plonsky went forward to post the sentries across the ravine where they linked up with the sailors at Flagstaff Bastion and the Minsk Regiment in Central Bastion. Unfortunately, during the night, fire from their own mortars killed one of them. They could hear work going on in the allied trenches, and a patrol of Cossacks on a raid passed through the outpost line. An N.C.O. of this patrol came back and reported that new allied trenches were being pushed forward. Going ahead with the N.C.O. to investigate, Hodasevich found, sure enough, a body of French troops entrenching. For a moment the two of them lay still as death, afraid to move, as the rattling of a firelock would at once have given the allies warning of their position. Finally, they went back having accomplished nothing, and soon afterwards the whole company were ordered to rejoin the remainder of the regiment in the reserve position at the Place du Théâtre in the town. Looking back, when dawn came, towards the position they had left, they saw puffs of smoke from shells from Russian

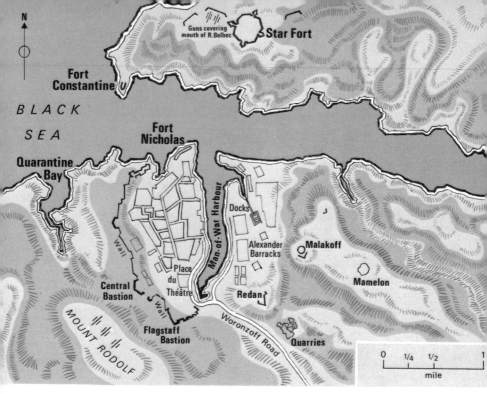

Sebastopol's fortifications

guns around the new French earthworks which they had inspected so closely during the night; then, as if in response, an
allied round shot pitched into the courtyard of a house near them
and killed two chickens. The allied bombardment had now begun.

A tremendous cannonade followed the arrival of that single
shot; and around them on the Place du Théâtre all was chaos. A
great number of soldiers, sailors, convicts and others were running for their lives through the streets. Asked what was the matter, their only answers were that the French had opened fire.
Hodasevich and his men hurried off to join the rest of the regiment
who they found had been ordered under arms to stop them running away. Indeed the unexpected opening of the allied bombardment seemed to have struck everyone with such panic that almost
all were ready to run to places of safety. The first killed and
wounded were now being carried away from the batteries, some
on stretchers, others in litters made of firelocks, and the dead in
sacks – the dead were taken over to the North Side to be buried.
It took some time before all the confusion that reigned throughout the town could be brought into order, and a proper fire began
from the batteries in retaliation; but eventually most of the
garrison were got back to their action stations.

Captain Hodasevich and his company were still left in the neighbourhood of the Place du Théâtre, and having nothing much to do, he went and joined the officers of the 3rd Battalion. Here he found also the colonel of the convict battalion, who appeared to have a good idea of what was happening. For example, he had noticed from a vantage point a ship with its yards and rigging in disorder off Quarantine Bay making as if for Eupatoria, and immediately concluded that this was a sign that some important personage of the allied fleet or army must be dead. Having heard that Marshal St. Arnaud had died, they thereupon correctly surmised that the vessel was carrying his remains to France.

About two in the afternoon, they noticed that the allied bombardment from the sea had begun; but the smoke around the town was so thick that they could not see the ships. The town at this time was a perfect hell, as from all sides shot was flying as thick as hail, and from the ships shells, round and cylindrical. These latter were objects of great respect and interest, and many of them that did not burst were carefully examined by the curious. The frightful din, smoke, groans and cries of the wounded as they were carried from the batteries, and the confusion that reigned, rendered the place the most horrible it was possible to conceive.

About three o'clock, the French powder magazine in Mount Rodolph was blown up by a shell from the Central Bastion, and there were loud shouts of joy throughout the town. The Russian commanders then organized a sortie of volunteers to destroy the battery and spike the guns. This force of three columns consisted of men from Hodasevich's regiment, sailors and convicts, and was led by Lieutenant Novikoff of the navy. It was thought the French battery on Mount Rodolph would be deserted after the explosion; but the attackers were soon disillusioned. As Novikoff with the centre column approached, a heavy rifle-fire opened on them. The flank columns next came under fire; and Hodasevich's company on the left under crossfire as well. As they looked like being cut off, these were withdrawn, and in fact only Novikoff with the centre column reached the battery. Finding in front of them a trench filled with riflemen, they too fled back; and so nothing was effected. Hodasevich lost nine men out of his party: two were left dead; but the wounded managed to crawl back. In retreat they had to run from outcrop of rock to outcrop, and then crouch. Directly they showed themselves, they were shot at.

The destruction done by the allied fleet seems to have been less than expected. Hodasevich says that even at Fort Constantine, which was most exposed, only twenty-seven were killed and wounded, and one gun disabled. That more damage was not done was probably because the allied ships were stationed at too great a distance out at sea.

About five o'clock, a large government magazine of flour near the Place du Théâtre was set on fire by a shell from the allied fleet. All the men that could be spared were sent to put it out under the energetic Lieutenant Novikoff who had only just returned from the sortie; but they only managed to save very little.

About six o'clock a rumour started to spread that Admiral Korniloff had been wounded while on his favourite vantage point on the Malakoff. It was said that his right leg had been shot away and there was little hope of saving his life. This was all passed from one to another in whispers, as it was forbidden to speak of it, for Korniloff was much respected and beloved by all belonging to the town of which he was regarded as the chief defender; and his death would have a very discouraging effect, especially on the sailors. He had done much already towards the preservation of the town by the coolness with which he conducted its defence. Many felt deep sorrow later when they heard of the death of this popular admiral. He was buried within the foundation of the new church near the library, where had been previously buried Admiral Lazareff who had commanded the Black Sea fleet before Korniloff.

They were all heartily glad when as the evening drew on, the allies ceased firing, for they had been pounded from six in the morning until seven in the evening. During the night they were undisturbed, and, in turns, took a little rest or repaired the damage done to the fortifications.

After the firing ceased, Hodasevich found that he had lost twenty men killed and wounded out of his company. The barracks behind Flagstaff Bastion were completely ruined, and in the bastion itself much of the breastwork had been demolished and the embrasures turned into gaping holes. But this was not very extraordinary, as they were not revetted, and the cheeks had been simply plastered with clay. In the Redan, the powder magazine was blown up killing forty men, and farther east still the tower of the Malakoff was ruined. It was a general view in the town that the English fired more accurately than the French; but the latter were handicapped by losing their magazine on Mount Rodolph.

There was little rest for Hodasevich's company that night, for he set half his men to work on repairing batteries and the other half making a shelter for themselves. By dawn next day most of the troops were back at their action stations ready for the renewal of the bombardment; but it was a special day for the Taroutine Regiment, as it was that of St. Thomas, their patron saint, an image of whom was always carried with them. About nine o'clock, most of the regiment were paraded on the Place du Théâtre to celebrate Holy Mass in the presence of the divisional general. The priest performed the sacred duty without giving the slightest heed to the shot continually whistling over and about him, though many were paying more attention to the direction in which the shot might pitch than the words of the priest. After mass the general went to the colonel's headquarters to drink success to the regiment and its future victories in sparkling champagne; and the colonel sent out ten bottles to the officers of each battalion. It must not be thought, however, that this was an act of spontaneous generosity, for the colonel had an entertainment allowance for the regimental holiday.

About eleven o'clock a great noise was heard on the Place du Théâtre; and a soldier came running back from the front line where a battalion of the regiment was still manning the wall between the Central and Flagstaff Bastions. 'The enemy are coming,' he shouted. The reserve companies were then ordered under arms and advanced to support their comrades on the wall. No sooner had Hodasevich given his company the order to advance, than, anxious to reach the safety of the wall, his men broke into a run, leaving him behind. It was a false alarm, however, and after waiting there a quarter of an hour, they returned. An hour later there was another alarm. This time Hodasevich, much to his men's annoyance, marched them towards the wall slowly in perfect order although under fire. Again it was a false alarm. Once more they returned to the Place du Théâtre.

On the third day of the bombardment the allies started to fire shell from their land batteries, their mortars not previously having been ready. In the confined streets of the town, the shells proved very destructive. Some of the defenders were daring enough to rush upon them as they fell, draw the fuse, and thus prevent them bursting, and saving the lives of their comrades. In the Russian forces anyone who did this successfully was awarded the Cross of St. George. This was much valued by the men, as its award exempted them from corporal punishment and gave them an increase of pay.

From 19 October the allies began to fire at night; but this did not worry the Russians unduly, as they could trace the course of the shells by their burning fuses. Besides, the firing was not at all rapid, and the lookout men could judge where they would land, right, left or behind. But when they were likely to be direct hits, it was all helter-skelter to find some place of safety. No lights were allowed in the town at night, or in the batteries, as that always afforded something for the allies to aim at, of which they were not slow to take advantage. The very soldiers were afraid to light their pipes lest they draw fire upon themselves. The people moved about the town as if afraid their footsteps would betray their presence to the enemy, and little was heard save the warning cries of the lookouts. At this stage they suffered most from rifle-balls which having been fired at great elevation fell almost perpendicularly on to the heads of men crowded behind the defences.

Colonel Todleben with a mounted orderly rode round daily to visit all the batteries of the town giving orders and directions as to what was to be done in repairs during the next night. His coolness and self-control was above praise. At each bastion there was an officer whose duty it was to watch the works of the enemy, and report daily their direction and progress to Todleben. Besides these, a tower had been built near the ladies' school, not very far from the library, where a constant lookout was kept. From all this information Todleben adjusted his own defences to meet the changing positions of the allies, and could concentrate a tremendous fire from his newly constructed batteries upon any given part of the allied trenches.

On 20 October, Hodasevich's battalion returned to their reserve station on the Place du Théâtre. Here they were safe from rifle-balls and had comfortable quarters in the houses near the theatre, including the home of the postmaster who had rushed out of the town in so great a hurry that he had left behind all his furniture and utensils, including a piano. Sometimes they would collect round this instrument, and while one played the rest would dance and sing, making so much noise that the whistling of the shot and shell could be no longer heard. All the firelocks were piled on the pavements, and one day several round shot rolled down the street and destroyed thirty weapons in Captain Hodasevich's company alone. One of his soldiers, while crossing the Place du Théâtre with a tin full of water, had a shell pitch within a few feet of him. He threw himself upon it, pulled out the fuse, and poured water into the hole. All this was watched by Hodasevich who was astounded at the man's bravery and great presence of mind. For this action the man later justly received the Cross of St. George. One evening, when Captain Hodasevich's men had just fallen in to go on fatigue duty to the batteries, and the sergeant was calling the master-roll, a shell pitched on the right flank of the company. The men began to run, but Hodasevich ordered them to lie down. Feeling ashamed to do likewise, before the whole company, he remained standing within a few yards of the spluttering shell in a state of mortal fear and wondering whether his time had come. However, to his great relief the fuse went out, and the danger was past. He ordered his men up again, and they began to move to the right when another shell came through the air with its peculiar chou-chouing, and pitched about three yards in front of the company. Some of the men threw themselves on the ground, but Hodasevich again remained standing, not knowing what to do, and thinking that having escaped one, the second would be

Colonel Todleben, hero of Sebastopol

sure to burst and single him out for its victim. Again, however, by a happy chance, the shell, like the former one, did not burst. The men got up again and went on to the battery. On the road later Hodasevich heard them talking over the two events that had just happened. They came to the conclusion that their captain was a wizard or enchanter; that if he said to a shell, 'burst not', it would not burst. They were convinced that he had the power of witchcraft. This is the way, according to Hodasevich, that a Russian soldier always explains what he cannot understand.

One day, when the regimental surgeon was having tea with the Catholic priest, a round shot burst through the ceiling of the room they were sitting in and fell on the head of the surgeon killing him on the spot, while the priest escaped unhurt. Soon afterwards, about six officers were sitting in the colonel's room after dinner when a shell broke through the roof, and the two stories above, into their room and burst before reaching the floor. Lieutenant Krasnik who was sitting near the window was killed by a splinter, and the others were nearly smothered in lime and plaster, and the room was filled with smoke. In the front room of the same house two cadets of the regiment were sitting reading near the window when a shell burst in the street, and a splinter flew into the room, and bouncing off the side of the window hit one of them in the cheek. Then it went on and struck an N.C.O. in the opposite corner in the chest, killing him on the spot. The cadet who was only eighteen died three hours later.

However, when Hodasevich's company was back in reserve in the town it lost only a few men, and the occurrences related above were exceptional. On the other hand, there was a good deal of sickness from diarrhoea brought on by the poor food, all of which was cooked up at Fort Nicholas and transported in large tubs to the batteries and reserve stations. It arrived quite cold, and with fat swimming in large cakes on the top of the soup was neither appetizing nor nourishing. Many men, according to Hodasevich, only kept going on their brandy, of which double portions were distributed morning and evening.

The Taroutine Regiment served inside Sebastopol throughout the first bombardment, after which it was relieved by the Ekatherinenburg Regiment and went off to join General Liprandi's force outside on the Tchernaya; but they did not reach the field army until after the battle of Balaclava.

From the 17th to the 20th heavy firing on both sides was kept up, the French once more joining in after putting matters to rights at

Mount Rodolph and getting up a fresh supply of ammunition. In the dark each night, however, the Russians set to work to repair their batteries, and they replaced the dismounted guns with others equally heavy. In fact, with large arsenals close at hand, they possessed many advantages over the besiegers; and these were made full use of by their able leaders, gallant old Admiral Korniloff and Colonel Todleben, the heroes of the defence of Sebastopol. The Russians also managed to concentrate a formidable force around Tchorgoun to the east of the Tchernaya; and the presence of this army known to be under General Liprandi, one of Russia's best commanders, constituted a threat not only to the British lines of communication, but to their base at Balaclava. This new Russian field army was soon to make its presence felt by a number of attacks on the British flank which have been named the Battle of Balaclava.

THE THIN RED LINE

✡

THE THIN RED LINE

*'The Russians charged in towards Balaclava. The
ground flew beneath the horses' feet; gathering speed
at every stride, they dashed on towards that thin red
line tipped with steel.'*

WILLIAM RUSSELL

Towards the end of the first bombardment of Sebastopol, the
British were concerned about Russian forces massing near
Tchorgoun beyond the Tchernaya. They feared their right flank
might be attacked at any time. This Russian army was put at
25,000, and Russian patrols were seen riding towards the British
cavalry outposts causing alarms and stand-tos in the cavalry
camps. Lord George Paget spoke of being turned out regularly
about midnight, but added, philosophically, that perhaps five
hundred false alarms were better than one surprise. Sir George
Cathcart was less restrained. He was already angry at the way
things were going – and never being consulted by Lord Raglan.
When he brought his division down from the plateau, and was then
told it was a false alarm, he nearly blew up with rage.

The immediate defences of Balaclava had not been neglected.
On the heights beyond the Genoese castle were 1,200 men of the
Royal Marines and Marine Artillery supported by two companies
of the 93rd under Major Gordon and a few detachments. The guns
were mostly 24-pounders, 32-pounders and 8-inch howitzers.
Lieutenant Roberts of the Royal Marine Artillery at No. 4
Battery on the heights wrote: 'On the evening of the 23rd, Sir
Colin Campbell (our commander here) sent for me and asked me
"like a good boy to go up the hill and superintend the formation of
a battery of three guns for the sake of an old fellow who had a great
deal of responsibility on his shoulders." The next day I went and
worked away with Highlanders and Turks till it was finished at
night and the guns in position.' The rest of the 93rd under Colonel
Ainslie guarded Balaclava from an attack from the north, occupying a hill near Kadikoi which barred the valley going down to the

107

harbour. They were supported by W Battery under Captain Barker and two and a half battalions of Turks.

The day after the 93rd's arrival, Surgeon Munro took possession of the church and priest's house at Kadikoi as a regimental hospital, and a house in the village as a hospital for officers. The church was locked and he felt a little compunction in breaking it open, but the necessity for having a place of shelter for his sick was urgent. On entering he saw several oil-paintings hanging on the eastern wall, and a small silver figure of the Dead Christ in a glass frame above the altar. Pictures and figure were all taken care of, and removed some time afterwards by the Q.M.G.'s department, and no doubt eventually restored to the Russians.

The local provost-marshal, although an officer of the 93rd, threatened to take both church and house from Munro because he had not got permission to occupy them; but as Munro doubted the real extent of the provost-marshal's authority, he went straight to Sir Colin Campbell who gave him an order to keep both. The majority of the officers and men of the regiment were suffering terribly at the time from bowel complaint and from skin eruptions attributable to long continued use of salt meat, want of vegetables and sleeping on bare ground; but the addition of grapes to their diet, and sleeping under the shelter of a roof, and on the dry wooden floors of the hospitals, was of benefit to the milder cases, though of little help to the more severe, many of whom died eventually of scurvy and scorbutic dysentery; while of the few they were able to send away to Scutari and to England some recovered, but never returned to the Crimea. For many weeks they had no hospital equipment, a very limited supply of medicines and nothing but ordinary rations. During the first half of the month the weather was pleasant; bright warm sunshine during the day was followed by a low temperature at night accompanied by heavy dews. Although the sudden alternations of temperature did not affect the strong and healthy, they were death to the weakly and sick. Realizing that some protection from the damp and chilly night air would help, Munro suggested the men should make shelter-huts for themselves with tendrils of the vines, or, failing this, that every two men should make a small tent with one blanket, a bed of vine leaves underneath it, and use the other blanket and their greatcoats as covering; but his suggestion was not followed by many as it was thought that tents might be issued at any moment, and in any case the stay in the Crimea would be short. This constant exposure cost Major Banner his life. He had been ill for some time, and should not have

108

been allowed to accompany the expedition. Assistant-Surgeon Sinclair was in charge at the time of embarkation from Varna and did not realize how bad Major Banner was, as he concealed the extent of his illness for fear of missing the campaign. When Munro was actually talking to him, he was struck down with cholera. He was carried to the medical tent nearby and laid down, still in his uniform, on a bed of straw. After several hours of great suffering he died. This was the second case of cholera in the 93rd since landing in the Crimea, but it was followed by several others which all proved fatal except for Lieutenant Clayhills. This was the same officer who nearly lost his life in the stream at Scutari, so he had two narrow escapes from death.

During the first half of October, details from the 93rd under Colonel Ainslie were employed every day in landing stores at Balaclava, and there was little military duty except to provide night-picquets. Meanwhile, the Turks were busy constructing and arming the redoubts along the Causeway Heights, and sailors from the fleet were helping the gunners move guns and ammunition past the 93rd camp at Kadikoi up on to the plateau.

In search of fresh food for his sick, Munro paid several visits to Balaclava to make friends with the commissariat. When the bombardment started, he jumped on his pony to go and see the fun. He was very disappointed. It had never occurred to him that it would be a complete failure. He returned day after day in the hope of seeing the assault and surrender, until at last it came to be generally expected that a further bombardment, perhaps a prolonged investment, would be necessary, and that winter would be spent in the Crimea. Tents were now issued, and the 93rd formed their camp on the southern slope of the hill on which they had been bivouacking. They were destined to remain there for the battle of Balaclava, and on into the next summer.

The main outer defences of the port were the redoubts along the Causeway Heights beside the Woronzoff Road between the North Valley and South Valley of Balaclava. As they guarded a valuable road up on to the Chersonese Plateau, it is surprising that they were only manned by Turks with a few British artillerymen as advisers. But although it was realized that the Turks were not very staunch in the open, because of their behaviour at the siege of Silistria in Bulgaria, it was believed they were good fighters behind defences.

No. 1 Redoubt, on what was later called Canrobert's Hill in honour of the new French commander, was situated at the east end of South Valley, and its three 12-pounders faced towards

Kamara. No. 2 Redoubt was just by the Woronzoff Road, and its two 12-pounders looked north-east towards the Tractir Bridge. Redoubts 3 and 4 had two 12-pounders each facing north across North Valley of Balaclava towards the Fedioukine Heights. Redoubts 5 and 6 were closer to the cliffs at the edge of the Chersonese Plateau, No. 6 being just south of where the road began to zigzag up on to the plateau. Neither 5 or 6 were armed. Along the edge of the cliffs was a line of French entrenchments with batteries up on the plateau behind. At the foot, at the west end of North Valley, were some Chasseurs d'Afrique from General d'Allonville's division of cavalry. At the west end of South Valley, just by No. 6 Redoubt, was a vineyard with the Light Brigade's camp to the east and the Heavy Brigade's camp to the south.

The Heavies now consisted of the 4th Dragoon Guards, the 5th Dragoon Guards, the Royals, the Scots Greys and the Inniskil-

General Scarlett, commander of the Heavy Brigade

lings; their commander was General Scarlett. The Light Brigade was made up of the 4th Light Dragoons, the 8th Hussars, the 11th Hussars, the 13th Light Dragoons and the 17th Lancers. They were commanded by Lord Cardigan, who, being out of sorts, was allowed to sleep on board his yacht *Dryad* in Balaclava harbour. He always dined aboard, and often made use of his privilege of sleeping there. Usually he could be seen cantering up to the Light Brigade camp about eleven o'clock each morning.

Lord Lucan was still in command of the cavalry division, and was a great deal more thorough than Lord Cardigan. Early every morning with his staff and Sir John Blunt his interpreter he rode down the South Valley of Balaclava to No. 1 Redoubt to have a look for himself at the Russians threatening his flank. He also sent out patrols with interpreters along the road to Kamara and Baidar to interrogate the local Tartars.

The 19th of October was a hard day for the British cavalry. They had just turned in from their early parade, when an orderly galloped from the outposts to say that Russian forces were approaching. Saddling up again, away they went up on to the Causeway between No. 4 and No. 5 Redoubts, and there, sure enough, were the Russians moving up towards them, about a mile away. C Troop R.H.A. under Captain Brandling opened up and sent over a few shots, but brushwood prevented their seeing the effect. However, it stopped the Russians coming forward. Although the cavalry remained on the ridge for several hours, from then on they saw only a few Russian vedettes scouting in the distance and at dusk their camp fires blazing.

Lord George Paget was one of the last to return to camp. While still on the ridge, he fell in with Sir Colin Campbell, and they walked down the hill into North Valley together. It was too dark to see much, but Sir Colin was most eager to find out exactly what was happening over in the enemy lines, and they lay down and put their ears to the ground to listen for Russian movements. Later, while they were returning together to the cavalry camps, they spoke of how the cavalry were being kept back out of the fight by Lord Raglan, and how the cavalry commander had been nicknamed Lord Look-on, because of it, by the rest of the army. Sir Colin said he was not worried about his own inaction, as he was not there primarily to fight a battle or gain a victory. His orders were to defend Balaclava, which was the key to the British position; and he was not going to be tempted out of it – all this in the broadest Scots accent and with the bluntness of an old soldier. They had to make their way through the Turkish lines on the

111

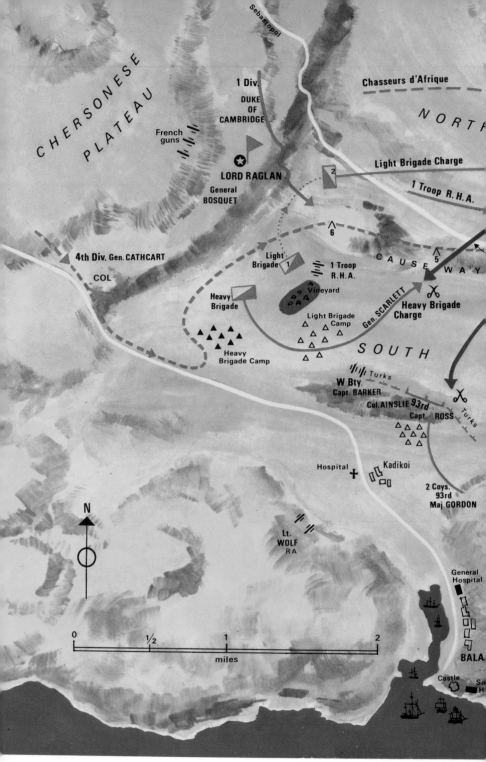

CHERSONESE PLATEAU

Sebastopol

1 Div.
DUKE OF CAMBRIDGE

Chasseurs d'Afrique

N O R T H

French guns

LORD RAGLAN

General BOSQUET

Light Brigade Charge

1 Troop R. H. A.

2

4th Div. Gen. CATHCART

COL

6

Light Brigade

1

1 Troop R.H.A.

C A U S E   W A Y

5

Vineyard

Heavy Brigade

Gen. SCARLETT

Heavy Brigade Charge

Light Brigade Camp

Heavy Brigade Camp

S O U T H

W Bty.
Capt. BARKER

Turks

Col. AINSLIE 93rd

Capt. ROSS

Turks

Hospital

Kadikoi

2 Coys. 93rd
Maj. GORDON

Lt. WOLF
R A

General Hospital

N

0   ½   1   2
miles

BALA

Castle   Sa   H

The field of Balaclava

UKINE
LLS

General
JABRUKRITZY

To Simpheropol

Aqueduct

R. Tchernaya

R. Chouliou

Cossacks

Tchorgoun

LEY

OIGAN

LUCAN

✂

General
RYJOFF

Russians

W Bty ⌄3

Cossacks

1 Troop
Greys

Woronzoff Road

2

General
LIPRANDI

IGHTS

Light & Heavy
Brigades
⎰ LUCAN
⎱ BLUNT
⎱ CAMPBELL

✂

1 > ✂

EY

Turks

CANROBERT'S
HILL

Kamara
+

arines

ALLIES

RUSSIANS

⌄4 The Redoubts
Armament:

No.1 : Three 12-Pounders

Nos. 2, 3 & 4 :
Two 12-Pounders each

Nos. 5 & 6 : unarmed

heights; and the Turks seeing them coming up in the dark from the front, whispered tremulously, 'Johnny?', and on receiving the reply, 'Buono Johnny!', seemed highly delighted. They heard them muttering to each other, 'Ah Johnny, buono Johnny, buono, buono.' Sir Colin said that he and Lord Lucan had had a conference with Liva (General) Rustem Pasha commanding the 4,000 Turks on the Causeway Heights, and found him extremely sensible and intelligent.

One hour before dawn on 25 October, the cavalry turned out as usual and waited in their lines while Lord Lucan with his staff and interpreter went off on their daily early morning reconnaissance to No. 1 Redoubt. They were still only going at a foot's pace when Lord George jogged off after them; but he stayed fifty yards behind the general with Lord William Paulet, the A.A.G., and Major McMahon, A.Q.M.G. They rode at a walk across the plain in the direction of Canrobert's Hill where the occupants of No. 1 Redoubt were in happy ignorance of the day's work in store. By the time they had approached to within 300 yards of the redoubt, the first faint streaks of daylight showed that the flagstaff on the redoubt flew two flags. 'Hallo,' said Lord William, 'there are two flags flying, what does that mean?' 'Surely it's the signal that the enemy is approaching,' said Major McMahon. 'Are you quite sure?' someone asked. They were not long kept in doubt. Hardly were the words out of McMahon's mouth, when bang went a cannon in the redoubt ahead firing on advancing masses of the enemy. Off scampered the two staff officers to their chief, and Lord George turned and galloped back as fast as he could to the Light Brigade, which he at once mounted on his own initiative as Lord Cardigan had not yet come up from his yacht.

Sir Colin Campbell had seen the party of officers riding across the front of the 93rd's position, and had jumped on his horse and trotted across to join Lord Lucan. They had a short consultation, after which Lord Lucan sent off A.D.C.s to warn Lord Raglan and bring up the cavalry brigades and horse artillery. Then they went forward to Canrobert's Hill to watch the Russian advance. This was marked by puffs of white smoke from shells from enemy guns in position near Kamara, increasing every moment and coming ever closer until the British leaders were under fire.

The Turks in No. 1 Redoubt, although greatly outnumbered, made a gallant stand at first, and both Lord Lucan and Sir Colin Campbell expressed their approval. 'Blunt,' Lord Lucan was heard calling to his interpreter, 'those Turks are doing well.' But having

Ismail Pasha and attendants

lost nearly half their number, and receiving no support, they retired, leaving their three guns, their killed and a few prisoners, mostly wounded, in the hands of the enemy. Seeing the Turks streaming down the hill to the rear, Blunt was sent to lead them off to form up with the 93rd at Kadikoi.

Blunt rode after the fleeing Turks and explained the orders to their bimbashi. Some of the men, parched with thirst and exhausted, gathered round him and began making complaints. One, faint and bleeding from a wound in his breast, asked why no support had been sent. Another said the guns in the redoubt were too small and ill-supplied with ammunition, some of which did not fit and could not be properly loaded. A third complained that during the last two days they had nothing to eat but biscuit and very little water to drink. Yet another, with his wounded head bandaged and smoking a pipe half a yard long, said to Blunt in Turkish,

115

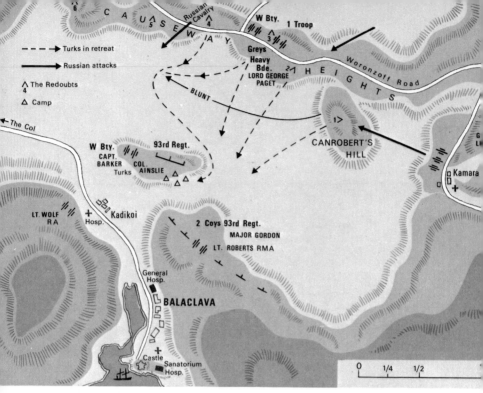

The flight of the Turks

'Neh Yappalim, Effendim? Allahim emrider' ('What can we do sir? It is God's will'). Then the bimbashi called the men away, and Blunt rode back to report to Lord Lucan.

Shortly after the Turks had been driven out of No. 1 Redoubt, those in 2, 3 and 4, numbering altogether about 800 men, seeing the large bodies of Russian cavalry and infantry advancing in their direction, and expecting no support, made but little resistance and fled towards Balaclava. As some stragglers from these redoubts were trudging along with their kits on their shoulders in the direction of the British cavalry camps at the west end of South Valley, Lord Lucan ordered Blunt again to go after them and turn them towards Kadikoi. Blunt had scarcely reached them when a regiment of Russian cavalry crossed the Woronzoff Road into South Valley. This was the force which later attacked the 93rd on the hill at Kadikoi.

Meanwhile, the Light Brigade under Lord George Paget advanced up South Valley as far as No. 2 Redoubt where they halted. Soon huge shot came lobbing like cricket-balls over the hill. They were mostly spent, and it was not difficult to avoid them; but this did not always hold good, for one of the first caught the horse of the front-rank left-flank man of the leading squadron of the 4th

116

Light Dragoons and completely whizzed him round. Lord George heard distinctly the slosh that sounded as it went through the centre of the animal's belly. Many were the shouts during the next half hour, 'Look out! Look out!' and exclamations at the narrow escapes of individuals. When Lord George was standing sideways on to No. 2 Redoubt, there were gesticulations and cries of 'Look out, Lord George!' Bewildered, he moved his horse on two or three paces. This had the effect of putting him into the line of the round shot they had seen coming, and which bounded actually between his horse's fore and hind legs throwing up a cloud of dust in his face. Standing in his conspicuous place, all eyes were on him, and few doubted the result as they saw the shot coming. But what a shout of congratulatory exhultation followed his escape, his first knowledge of which was his orderly's rollicking comment, 'Ah, ha! it went right between your lordship's horse's legs!'

While the Light Brigade had halted behind No. 2. Redoubt, the Heavy Brigade had moved farther forward, and I Troop R.H.A. under Captain Maude had advanced towards a point a little to the right of where No. 3 Redoubt crowned the Causeway Heights. Breasting the slope at a gallop, I Troop dropped swiftly into action. The level rays of the rising sun, now well above the horizon and smiting directly in the faces of the detachments, stopped them seeing the enemy. There were, however, flashes in the mist that hung over the hillsides, which indicated a long line of guns at the end of North Valley whose fire seemed to be directed mainly at No. 3 Redoubt. I Troop opened at once on the flashes; but all it did was to attract the attention of the Russian gunners from the redoubt to the British 6-pounders standing out on the skyline. The enemy fire became hot, and the horses of the detachments were withdrawn behind the reverse slope of the Causeway, where the Greys, who had been detached to support the guns, were drawn up. The limbers were still serving the guns with their teams hooked in facing the rear. They were under a merciless rain of shot and shell, and five horses of No. 6 gun's limber were struck down, as well as several spokes being knocked out of limber wheels. Lieutenant F. T. Whinyates said the men around the guns seemed to bear charmed lives, for although the gun carriages were scored and injured by the shell which burst among them, and this was especially the case in the left half-troop, yet the round shot passed harmlessly over and between the sub-divisions, and at this period there were no casualties of any consequence amongst the gunners, though there were some remarkably narrow escapes.

117

I Troop had been in action some fifteen to twenty minutes when Captain Maude, whilst calling attention to the advance of some grey-coated infantry skirmishers coming up through the brushwood, and directing the howitzers to open fire on them with shrapnel, had his horse killed by a shell, which bursting at the moment of impact brought him to the ground badly maimed in an arm and leg and wounded in the face. A tourniquet which he fortunately had in his holsters was placed on his arm, the artery of which was lacerated, and four men carried him on a limber blanket to the rear. The command of the troop now devolved on Lieutenant Dashwood who was senior to Whinyates, the other subaltern present. He at once mounted his horse, but it was soon killed by a round shot. Barely was he in the saddle of a second when that too was shot. It was at this juncture that Lord Lucan rode up. Realizing that the troop was being overpowered by the Russians guns and assaulted by infantry as well, and that nearly every round in its limbers had been expended, and seeing dead on the field a third of its gun horses, he gave orders to limber up and withdraw down South Valley. As the troop retired, a round shot killed Gunner McBride of No. 4 sub-division, knocking him clean out of his saddle. This shot also killed the two centre horses of No. 4 gun.

Sir Colin Campbell had ordered W Battery to support the redoubts, and Captain Barker took his guns away from the 93rd's position up on to the Causeway Heights. I Troop was already in the best position on the right of No. 3 Redoubt, so Captain Barker went over to the left where there was only a field of fire across North Valley towards the Fedioukine Hills, and they could not reach the Russians attacking Nos. 1 and 2 Redoubts. When I Troop got knocked about and was retired, Captain Barker, on orders from Sir Colin, sent Lieutenant Dickson with two guns of W Battery to take over their position. But they did not stay long in this vulnerable spot. Seeing they were likely to be overrun, Sir Colin ordered the whole of W Battery back to Kadikoi. Stopping and firing as they went, they reached the 93rd's position again. At one stage in the withdrawal Dickson tried to use his rockets, but a round shot killed a wheel horse of the rocket carriage, and it only got away with great difficulty, and could not wait to reply. Back in its old position at Kadikoi, W Battery's fire was again restricted. They could fire straight ahead, but were obstructed by the 93rd's hill and could not cover a direct attack on the Highlanders' position. However, they shot up the Russian cavalry on the Causeway Heights as did the Marine Artillery and

118

Lieutenant Wolf's battery on the hills behind. Surgeon Munro saw 'two of Wolf's shells burst beautifully close to the centre of the Russian column so that they retired for a time to the north of the Causeway Heights.' Less happily, one of the Inniskillings' horses was killed by a shot from W Battery.

Lieutenant Roberts of No. 4 Battery on the Marine Heights was woken early that morning by troops alongside rushing to get under arms. Jumping from his straw bed he ran off to his observation post where he saw the Russians attacking the Turkish-held redoubts on the far side of South Valley. He could see also the Russian guns in action by Kamara village, and remarked that their practice was 'exceedingly good'. With disgust he noticed that as the Russians ascended one side of Canrobert's Hill, the

Sir Colin Campbell

119

Turks 'streamed down the other'. Whilst this was going on, the ubiquitous Sir Colin arrived and ordered Roberts to form a breast-work in a ditch in front of the Turkish camp near him and to post the rest of their battalion in front of No. 3 Battery. While so engaged, Russian shot and shell was directed at them, but fell about 200 or 300 yards short. Returning to No. 4 Battery, Roberts saw the British cavalry and horse artillery retiring under fire, and the shell-burst which disabled Captain Maude. The Russian cavalry was by this time offering a good target, and Roberts personally supervised the fire from his 24-pounders, 32-pounders and 8-inch howitzers, rushing about from one gun to another seeing the fuses bored and laying the guns. The shells burst all among the Russians, and where they fell, 'horses were seen to reel and fall with their riders', so that Roberts was convinced that No. 4 Battery's practice was 'most admirable'.

Meanwhile, the Heavy Brigade, except the Greys, had been trying to protect the Turks streaming away in disorderly flight from the redoubts, and afterwards in checking the advance of a body of the enemy which threatened to issue down the valley between the redoubt and the village of Kamara. When, however, the brigade began to get knocked about by fire from the Russian batteries, it received orders to retire towards the cavalry camps. It was at this moment that the Greys and the remnants of I Troop came down from the Causeway and were directed to form a line and cover the retreat of the rest of the Heavy Brigade. This movement was executed with great steadiness, the Greys falling back by alternate squadrons and the guns by half-troops, though the latter had yet more horses killed or disabled by fire from Canrobert's Hill and its vicinity.

When the defence line across South Valley was as far back as Kadikoi, I Troop was met by Captain Shakespear, with the first-line wagons, and he replenished the exhausted limbers and took over command. As battery captain he had gone with the wagon horses as usual early that morning to Balaclava to help transport siege material to the Sebastopol front, but anxious about the continuous firing to the east had returned to the cavalry camps, hooked in and brought the wagons into South Valley. The limbers having been filled and various casualties made good, I Troop, under orders from Lord Raglan, went back with the Cavalry Division to the hilly ground near No. 6 Redoubt. Here they were close under the cliffs of the Chersonese Plateau, and could see very little in any direction.

The opening scenes of the battle of Balaclava were watched by

Surgeon Munro from the hill at Kadikoi. When the Turks were driven out of No. 1 Redoubt, those holding 2, 3 and 4 retired also, and all to the number of about a thousand came streaming across South Valley pursued by Russian cavalry, the first squadrons of which Sir John Blunt had noticed. They came in the direction of the 93rd who were drawn up in line on the crest of the hill above the regimental camp. With the 93rd stood a few men of the Rifle Brigade, some invalids, including a man or two from the Guards, sent up from Balaclava under Captain Inglis, and a battalion of Turks on either side. As soon as the Turks had abandoned the redoubts, a large body of Russian infantry appeared over the causeway. These were accompanied by artillery which immediately opened fire on the Highlanders causing several casualties. Two men in the centre company were wounded; one of them, Charles McKay, had his foot and ankle shattered by a round shot, and the other was wounded in the knee by a fragment of shell. Several Turks were also wounded. Sir Colin, noticing these casualties, ordered the 93rd to fall back under cover of the reverse slope of the hill. All this was quickly and quietly done; but it unsettled the Turks on either side, some of whom began to pull away altogether from the position and make off towards Balaclava, joining up with the Turks running away from the redoubts. It should be noted, however, that the thirty Turks attached to W Battery continued at their posts throughout the action.

Mrs. Duberly was a witness of the flight of the Turks. Feeling far from well, she had decided to remain quietly on board that day, but on looking through her stern cabin windows saw her horse saddled and waiting on the quay in charge of their soldier servant on the pony. A moment later, a note was put into her hands from Henry. It said: 'The battle of Balaclava has begun, and promises to be a hot one. I send you the horse. Lose no time, but come as quickly as you can; do not wait for breakfast.'

Duly impressed, Mrs. Duberly dressed in haste, went ashore without delay and, mounting Bob, started off for the Light Brigade camp as fast as the narrow and crowded streets of Balaclava would allow. She was hardly clear of the town, when she met a commissariat officer who told her that the Turks had abandoned the redoubts and were running towards the town. He begged her to keep as much to the left as possible, and to lose no time in getting to the camp as a large Russian force was upon them, adding, 'For God's sake, ride fast, or you may not reach the camp alive.' Turning off on to the grass beside the track, the old horse stretched into his stride, and they soon reached the main road and

The Thin Red Line

clattered towards the camp. The road was almost blocked with fleeing Turks: some unencumbered, running hard and yelling, 'Ship, Johnny! Ship, Johnny!' others, laden with pots, kettles and plunder of all descriptions, but chiefly old bottles for which they had a great liking. They poured through the 93rd's camp; but they got short shrift there. Mrs. Smith, the wife of Private Smith, a soldier-servant of Quartermaster Sinclair, saw to that. She set upon the first Turk who entered her tent – she probably thought he had come either to steal or take liberties with her. 'A large powerful bony [with one n] woman', she took hold of his collar and kicked him out. This exploit made her into something of a celebrity in the army. As a compliment they all called her Kokana Smith, Kokana being the Turkish word for woman.

Arriving at the cavalry camp, Mrs. Duberly looked back and saw the 93rd drawn up on the hill by Kadikoi, and Turks pursued by mounted Cossacks streaming away towards the port. Henry was standing by their tent, and, on her arrival he quickly struck it and packed up their things. Seizing a pair of laden saddle-bags, a greatcoat and two loose packages, Mrs. Duberly jumped the ditch into the vineyard behind the camp and waited for her husband. Here, having loaded Whisker the pony, Henry joined her; then they made their way up on to the Chersonese plateau to safety.

When the cavalry appeared over the Causeway in front of the 93rd's position, a detachment of 400 rode down into the valley making as if for Balaclava. At first they came at the trot, but soon increased their pace. When it became certain that they were coming towards the 93rd, Sir Colin ordered the regiment to reform line on the forward crest of the hill, saying, before they did so, 'There is no retreat from here, men! You must die where you stand!' To which John Scott, the right-hand man of Lieutenant Burrough's company replied, 'Ay, ay, Sir Colin; and needs be we'll do that!'

Just as the 93rd were reforming, the two companies under Major Gordon arrived from the Marine Heights and joined the line. A Pole attached to W Battery had been sent off to call them back to Kadikoi; and he had gone most unwillingly. He had been afraid of missing the battle and the opportunity of revenge on the hated Russians.[1] However, he got back in plenty of time, and with

---

1. *After the battle he found the corpse of a Russian trooper out in front with bullet wounds which he said had not been made by a minié, and he claimed this victim as his.*

his double-barrelled gun at the ready took his place in the line among the Highlanders.

Having formed line on the crest, the 93rd stood steady and silent, eyeing the approaching cavalry and wondering what they were going to do. The war correspondent William Russell was watching from the edge of the Chersonese plateau, and described this dramatic moment in the battle. He wrote: 'The silence was oppressive; between the cannon bursts one could hear the champing of bits and clink of sabres in the valley below. The Russians drew breath for a moment, and then in one grand line charged in towards Balaclava. The ground flew beneath their horses' feet; gathering speed at every stride, they dashed towards that thin red streak tipped with steel.' The sight of the charging horsemen did not disturb the Highlanders, but it unsettled most of the remaining Turks, and, after firing a volley, they turned, broke ranks and bolted through the 93rd's camp towards Balaclava.

As the Russians came closer, the 93rd showed a mind to rush forward and charge them. Sir Colin would have none of that. In an instant he was heard calling out to them fiercely, 'Ninety-third! Ninety-third! damn all that eagerness!' and the angry voice of their old commander quickly steadied the line. At last, however, when the squadrons were within minié range, the order came to fire, and the Highlanders delivered their volleys. They quickly emptied two saddles, and hit many other men; these were seen clinging wounded to their mounts, many of whom were also disabled.

The Highlanders' volleys took the impetus from the charge. The Russians first slackened speed, and then led towards their left, as if to ride round the Highlanders' flank. Sir Colin watched this move with interest. Turning to his A.D.C.,[1] and speaking of the officer who led the Russian squadrons, he said, 'Shadwell! that man understands his business.' But the Highlanders were a match for the Russian squadrons, for Captain Ross's grenadier company faced round towards the horsemen and poured volley after volley into their flank. This was the end. Stopped by Ross's quick manoeuvre, the squadrons wheeled again to their left, and retreated. They retreated together, but not in good order; and as they moved over the Causeway to safety, shots from W Battery

---

1. Later the A.D.C., Captain Shadwell, wrote a biography of Sir Colin Campbell.

increased their confusion. The battle over, there came a burst of cheering from the victorious 93rd whose staunchness had saved Balaclava.

At Alma, Captain Hodasevich wondered how men could be found brave enough to attack in such thin lines; also at Alma, Lord Raglan had exclaimed, 'Look how well the Highlanders advance!' Now at Balaclava, William Russell likened them, while waiting to receive the Russians' charge, to 'a thin red streak tipped with steel'. For these glorious exploits the 93rd became, from that day forward, 'The Thin Red Line'.

THE CHARGE OF
THE HEAVY BRIGADE

THE CHARGE OF
THE HEAVY BRIGADE

*'A particularly vicious-looking Russian trooper with
a large blue nose and savage glittering eye managed
to strike Lieutenant Elliot on the forehead, while at
the same time another divided his face with a deep-
slashing wound. Hacked at and struck at again and
again, and by this time completely dazed, he nevertheless managed miraculously to leave the mêlée still in
the saddle. It is strange that although wounded
fourteen times, he was returned in despatches later as
only "slightly wounded".'*

KINGLAKE

The cavalry had hardly returned to the west end of the valley,
before the Heavy Brigade[1] was ordered back again to support the
Highlanders at Kadikoi. The Light Brigade, now under Lord
Cardigan, remained in the undulating ground beside No. 6 Redoubt, where their view was limited, while General Scarlett led
the Heavies round the vineyard and through their own camp site
to carry out this new assignment. Lord Raglan's order had suggested eight squadrons; but the whole brigade, led by the Inniskillings and Scots Greys, and well strung out, moved round the
vineyard to the neighbourhood of the Light Brigade's camp, where
most of the tents had already been struck following the panic after
the Russians' first assault on No. 1 Redoubt.

General Scarlett was quite unconscious of the presence of
Russian cavalry on the Causeway, and took the head of his
force round to the front of the vineyard without sending out
scouts or taking any precautions against surprise. Riding ahead
with Lieutenant Elliot, his elderly A.D.C., on the left of the
column formed by one squadron of Inniskillings and two of Greys,
his whole attention was directed on the Highlanders at Kadikoi,

1. *The Heavy Brigade consisted of Dragoon Guards and Dragoons who were mounted
on bigger, stronger horses than were the Lancers, Light Dragoons and Hussars of the
Light Brigade.*

129

Camp of the 4th Dragoon Guards, a convivial party of French and English

when Elliot, looking back, saw that beside the unmanned No. 5 Redoubt the top of the ridge was 'fretted with lances'. Elliot touched his general's arm, and pointed up at the Russian squadrons now silhouetted on the skyline; and Scarlett's reaction was instantaneous. Realizing that he was marching an unorganized force across the front of a mass of enemy cavalry about to charge, he decided to get in first. Facing his horse towards the flank of the column, he gave the order: 'Left wheel into line.' The 5th Dragoon Guards were just behind; the 4th Dragoon Guards and Royals were approaching; hoping that these would join in the charge on their arrival, he prepared to lead his first 300 men against the enemy – Scarlett's 'Three Hundred', they came to be called.

Just at this moment, Lord Lucan arrived. Warned by an A.D.C. sent from Lord Raglan that General Ryjoff's cavalry were advancing *en masse*, he had told Lord Cardigan to remain where he was, and galloped off to warn General Scarlett. As he approached, he told the regiments in the rear to wheel into line, thereby reinforcing Scarlett's orders; and then he rode up to confer in person with the Heavy Brigade's commander. He agreed with Scarlett's plan to attack, and even made it his own by saying, 'General Scarlett, take these squadrons, and at once attack the column of the enemy.'

General Scarlett was raring to go – as was General Lucan to see him gone, but the officers of the Inniskillings and Greys considered it necessary to dress their men properly before a charge. Possibly in view of the ineffectiveness of piecemeal attacks, they were right. But to the spectators on the cliffs, it appeared as if a formal drill parade was being carried out in the face of the enemy. It seemed that an opportunity was being lost, for, as they conscientiously dressed the ranks of their men, the officers presented their backs to the Russians who, with trumpets sounding, were pouring down the hill.

Well in front of the first line were General Scarlett and Lieutenant Elliot. Elliot was a veteran of campaigns in India, and preferred to fight in comfort. He had come out earlier in his forage cap; but Scarlett had quickly sent him back for the cocked-hat he should wear as a staff officer, muttering, 'My staff shall be properly dressed.' The Inniskillings were ready first; and Lord Lucan then impatiently ordered his divisional trumpeter to sound the charge, but no one paid the least attention; for the officers of the Greys were still facing their men and waiting for the senior major to bring them round with the order, 'Eyes right!'

At last, however, all was ready. Scarlett first sent off his brigade-major to bring forward the regiments behind, and tell them to attack the enemy's flanks; then, as still 'no attention was being awakened by the sound of the divisional trumpet', he ordered his own trumpeter to sound the charge. On this, the horsemen bounded forward, but in spite of all their dressing they got off to a ragged start, for those on the left were impeded by the pegs and ropes of tents of the Light Brigade camp.

Fortunately for the Heavy Brigade, the Russians had slackened their pace. After shaking themselves out for the conflict, sending out flanking screens of skirmishers, and throwing forward two wings, they had come to a halt. This lost them the chance of sweeping down like a torrent on the British; but their two antennae-like arms could now move in and crush any frontal attack, while the massed ranks of horsemen in their two main bodies behind presented a formidable obstacle to an attack from any direction.

The appearance of the two adversaries was strikingly different. Most of the Russians, whether Cossacks, hussars or lancers, officers or troopers, wore shakos and were enveloped in long murky grey overcoats, which looked almost black to Kinglake and the other spectators on the edge of the Chersonese plateau. The English dragoons on the other hand were in scarlet, with the

131

Greys in their bearskins and the rest in helmets. The contrast of colour between the grey and the red was so strong that the movements of the attackers could be easily followed by the spectators on the cliffs.

While the trumpet was still being sounded, Scarlett moved forward, and after threading his way carefully among the tent ropes, he reached open ground and galloped off, followed by Elliot and his trumpeter, straight at the enemy mass in front. He soon left the Greys behind, and turning partly round in his saddle, shouted, 'Come on, Greys!' waving them forward with his sword. They did their best to catch up, but like the Inniskillings on the right, who had a clearer passage, they were still about fifty yards behind their leader when he reached the enemy column.

At the spot near the centre at which Scarlett rode, a Russian officer was sitting on his horse out in front. Seeing Elliot's cocked-hat, and believing him the senior, the Russian allowed Scarlett to pass and turned instead on his A.D.C. He faced Elliot as he approached, and endeavoured to cut him down. Parrying the cut, Elliot drove his sword through the Russian's body, and so fast was he travelling, that the blade went right in up to the hilt. It stuck fast and dashing past, still gripping the hilt tightly, he could not withdraw it. Not until the Russian officer was turned round in his saddle by the leverage of the sword did he manage to pull it out reeking with blood.

Meanwhile, Scarlett had driven his charger in between the two nearest troopers, and wedged himself into the solid mass of the enemy's horsemen, some of whom jumped off their horses before he struck at them. Scarlett was only a passably good swordsman, and had the disadvantage of being near-sighted; but by keeping his blade whirling on both sides in quick succession, he carved a path for himself through the enemy. Turning towards the right, he eventually emerged with only minor wounds on the east flank of the column.

Elliot came out of the charge less happily than his general. Perhaps because of his conspicuous cocked hat, the Russians set on him with great determination. For a time, his skill as a swordsman and the uncommon length of his blade enabled him to ward off all attacks. In this his charger helped. Upset by being pressed on all sides, the animal lashed out with its heels to such good effect that it cleared a space behind its master. However, this did not dispose of his assailants in front; and a particularly vicious looking Russian trooper, with a large blue nose and savage glittering eye, managed to strike him in the forehead,

132

while, at the same time another, who had avoided the horse's heels, divided his face with a deep-slashing wound. Hacked at and struck at again and again, and by this time completely dazed, he nevertheless managed miraculously to leave the mêlée still in the saddle. It is strange that although he was wounded fourteen times, he was returned in despatches later as only 'slightly wounded'. Nor was his bravery recognized officially. Although most strongly recommended by General Scarlett for an award, Lord Lucan struck his name from the list because he was only a staff officer. Nor could he, it was said, be named for the Victoria Cross 'because what he did was no more than his duty'. To make matters worse Lord Lucan named in his despatches, at the exclusion of Elliot, his own A.D.C. who had not even been in the charge!

The regiments of the Scots Greys and Inniskilling Dragoons had been firm friends since they fought together in the Union Brigade at Waterloo, but they were dissimilar in character. The 'Skins had still some remaining traces of Orange enthusiasm, and were 'eager, fiery and impetuous'; the Scots Greys on the other hand loved a fight, but were more restrained: thus, while the 'Skins entered the fray with a cheer, the Greys merely let forth a fierce moan of rapture. The Russians were not entirely mute either. Although they abstained from yelling, they uttered as they fought a deep gurgling long-drawn sound, a kind of sustained continuous 'zizz' made with clenched teeth, resembling the sound of wheels humming and buzzing in a factory.

Besides outnumbering the British by ten to one, the Russians had some advantage in protective clothing. The British were without their shoulder-scales and gauntlets, and their serge red jackets were relatively thin, whereas the material of the Russians' coarse long grey overcoats was thick enough to protect them against sabre cuts except when made with great force. On the other hand, the Russians were either hussars or other light cavalry, and the red-coated troopers had the advantage of weight in men and horses, were higher off the ground, and had a longer reach with their sword-arms. Also, although the Russians had only initially the task of overwhelming or shaking off a mere 300 assailants, they were handicapped by being wedged together in two large masses and could not make full use of their superiority in numbers.

As the British approached, some of the Russians raised their carbines and fired, and Colonel Griffith of the Greys was killed; but these were soon put aside, and the matter was settled with cold steel. The next to enter the enemy mass was Colonel Dalrymple White of the Inniskillings. Well to the right of Scarlett, he too cut his way successfully into the enemy column and although badly wounded got out alive. Scarlett's 'Three Hundred' crashed in so weightily that no cavalry extended in line and halted could have withstood the shock; but as the Russian front-rank men were held by the massed ranks behind, they had to stay. Unwilling, however, to remain in front of charging Britishers, they, as it is said, 'accepted the files', easing sideways and letting the troopers in among them. In some parts of the column the combatants were for a time completely wedged, and could not move their horses in any direction. Then by whirling their sabres round and round overhead, and seizing any chance of a thrust or cut which presented itself, the redcoats managed to push on into the column. Their horses ducked instinctively, and left free scope for the

5th Dragoon Guards Rough-rider Macnamara

Major Burton and officers of the 5th Dragoon Guards

sabre work above them. As the sabres often rebounded like a cudgel from the thick grey overcoats of the Russians, there was little bloodshed; but, nevertheless, the redcoats pushed farther and farther in; and some of the Russians even turned their horses to face the rear with thoughts now of retreat. From the time the 'Three Hundred' closed, there was little use of fire-arms and the only sounds were from the clash of sabres and jangle of accoutrements.

After the 'Three Hundred' had charged, the other squadrons of the Heavy Brigade entered the fray. According to the watching Lord Lucan, the whole battle only took eight minutes, and the remaining charges were more or less simultaneous. The 5th Dragoon Guards prolonged the line of Scarlett's 'Three Hundred', and came in a little after them on their left. Meanwhile, the other squadron of the Inniskillings charged and met the east-projecting wing, while the Royals struck the west-projecting wing; and both these charges frustrated to some extent the Russian manoeuvre of pressing in their wings and crushing Scarlett's men in the rear. Finally, on Lord Lucan's orders, the 4th Dragoon Guards, led by Colonel Hodge, advanced along the edge of the vineyard and struck the Russian flank.

The 5th Dragoon Guards were slowed up by having to pass through the Light Brigade Camp, and by the time they joined in the Russian wing was moving obliquely on the rear of the Greys. This resulted in a terrible mix-up. There were Greys and Russians, and then more Russians moving in with the 5th Dragoon Guards in their rear. However, many Russians were unhorsed by the 5th's

135

136   *The 6th Inniskilling Dragoons at the Battle of Balaclava*

charge. Troopers of the Heavies were not the only ones involved in this area. Several men on duty in the camps joined in. These included two butchers who leapt on horses left sick in the lines and entered the fray in their shirt sleeves, swinging their swords as if they were meat-cleavers. A few from the Light Brigade also arrived. Avoiding the gaze of their officers, they slunk away and joined the fight.

The other squadron of the Inniskillings under Captain Hunt on the right had good galloping ground in front; and as, when they struck the Russian wing, it had just completed its wheel inwards, they hit the Russians in their backs, off guard. Piercing their line like an arrow, Captain Hunt shot through followed by his squadron; and the shock on the rear of the wheeling horsemen was so great that they were either tumbled from their horses or were driven forward on the front ranks in confusion.

One of the last regiments to arrive were the Royals. Coming past the south end of the vineyard just when Scarlett's men had completed their charge, they saw the Greys on their conspicuous mounts being buried in the mass as the Russian wing folded inwards on to them. Anxious and eager to help, the cry went up, 'By God, the Greys are cut off. Gallop! gallop!' Then to a cheer, with trumpets sounding, and ranks imperfectly formed in their haste, they charged and struck the Russians' in-wheeling line. But they were less successful than the Inniskillings on the right had been. Catching only the tip, they got thoroughly mixed up with the Russians there, and the rest of the wing managed to close in on the rear of the Greys unscathed. Troop Sergeant Major Norris of the Royals was a little behind the rest and, hurrying to join his comrades, was set on by four Russian hussars. He proved himself their equal. Killing one with a cut from his sabre, he drove off the rest. Then taking hold of the slain man's charger by the bridle, he rejoined his regiment. This, however, was in a confused state and had given up any immediate plan to reach the Greys who were now rallying to fight their way out of the mêlée. The Royals could hear them doing this. Above the din of battle, they could hear the voice of Captain Miller the adjutant crying, 'Rally the Greys'. Mounted on his vast white charger, and famous for his loud word of command, the men of the regiment not only heard him, but were able to pick him out. Although the task of rallying seemed impossible, their own determination to obey orders and the weight of their mighty grey horses cleared a way through the thicket of enemy squadrons; and rally they did. Moving towards the adjutant as he ordered them to face him, they came slowly together out of the

138

press. While the Greys were rallying, the Royals rallied too; for before leading his men forward again, Colonel Yorke had now decided they must be reformed.

Meanwhile, the 4th Dragoon Guards were making their charge under Colonel Hodge on the west flank of the Russian main body; and this proved the most successful of them all, for Colonel Hodge fought his way from flank to flank followed by his troopers.

The enemy columns and wings had now been pierced and shattered by all the regiments of the Heavy Brigade in turn. It was as if a number of crowbars had been thrust into the mass and then turned and twisted to wrench and shatter, and destroy, and the combined efforts began to take effect. The Russians started to back, and face towards the rear, and then to break ranks, and finally to, retreat. Eight minutes after Scarlett had ordered the charge, they were making off over the Causeway in confusion, followed by shots from I Troop with the Light Brigade, and from W Battery at Kadikoi.

The charge of the Heavy Cavalry at Balaclava

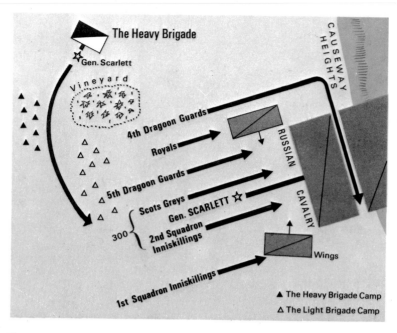

How the Heavy Brigade made their attack

The watchers on the edge of the cliffs, and the Light Brigade drawn up in the rear, had followed the whole short encounter with amazement. They had seen Scarlett and his staff, and his first 'Three Hundred', and finally the other regiments, charge, and get engulfed and lost in the Russian columns; but then, suddenly, they had discovered they were able to follow the redcoats threading their way through the grey mass. With their glasses, they could even pick out some of the officers: Captain Miller, for example, on his great horse rallying the Greys; and Scarlett with his red face and big moustache fighting like a madman. They saw the two Russian columns heave, swing and surge this way and that, and the wings in-wheel to crush the 'Three Hundred'; and they feared for their comrades. 'How can such a handful survive, much less make headway against such a legion?' wondered Lord George. 'They seem surrounded, and must be annihilated. One hardly dares to breathe.' However, at the sight of the Russians retreating, this mood changed. Now the watchers threw their hats in the air, and burst into cheers.

When their opponents disappeared over the Causeway, the

140

troopers below stood as if dazed, their tired sword-arms hanging loose at their sides, their hands and uniform spattered with blood. Then they pulled themselves together and started bearing away the wounded to the tents in the camp beside the vineyard. While this was in progress, an A.D.C. from Lord Raglan rode up to General Scarlett and handed him a message. It read simply, 'Well done!' Others also paid their tributes to the gallantry of the Brigade. Sir Colin Campbell galloped across from Kadikoi and joined a group of battle-worn Greys. Raising his bonnet in salutation, he exclaimed in a voice charged with emotion, 'Greys! gallant Greys! I am sixty years old, but if I were young again I would be proud to ride in your ranks.'

The Heavies had seventy-eight killed and wounded in this conflict, and the Russians, according to British reckoning, still

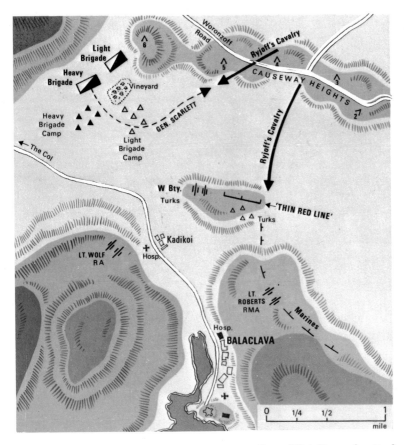

General Ryjoff's cavalry attack

141

more; but protected as they were by their heavy overcoats, and by shakos which even an axe blow could not split, this disparity cannot have been great. It was a brilliant victory; but not a complete one as the Russians were allowed to escape, and for this the Light Brigade is often held responsible. They had, however, been told to stay where they were; and Lord Cardigan knew that Lord Raglan wished to keep, as he said, his cavalry 'in a bandbox' for a real emergency. Lord Cardigan had suffered in Bulgaria from acting on his own initiative. Now he was fully determined to carry out Lord Lucan's and Lord Raglan's orders to the very letter. He was told to stay put, and stay he would, whatever the consequences. Because of this, except for the stragglers who dashed off to join in, and I Troop under Captain Shakespear, which dropped into action and sent a few shells after the enemy, the Light Brigade played no part in the battle. The most frustrated was Captain Morris in temporary command of the 17th Lancers. He had the temerity to point out to his irascible commander the splendid opportunity he was missing of charging a fleeing enemy; but Lord Cardigan was adamant. 'No,' he replied, 'we have been ordered to remain here.' Lord George agreed with this decision, but not for the same reason. He thought the ground in front too rough for an effective charge; and that the Russians were not in the state of disorder that Captain Morris believed.

The charge of the Heavy Brigade at Balaclava was a great achievement; but because of the lack of pursuit, the Russian horse did not suffer such discomfiture as to make it a classic victory. It was disappointing. Disappointing for Lord Raglan who was responsible because he held the light cavalry in check through his 'bandbox' principle; disappointing for Lord Lucan who considered his orders allowed Lord Cardigan to participate bearing in mind the wonderful opportunity; and disappointing above all for Lord Cardigan because of the jealousy engendered from watching the Heavies' success and not feeling able to share in it. He did not hide this. 'Damn those Heavies,' he repeated constantly. 'They have the laugh of us to-day.'

THE CHARGE OF
THE LIGHT BRIGADE

✡

THE CHARGE OF
THE LIGHT BRIGADE

'Never mind, my lord; we are ready to go again.'

A TROOPER AFTER THE CHARGE

The charge of the Heavy Brigade ended the second period of the battle, and changed its course, for the Russians who had been prevented from reaching Balaclava by the 93rd had now been completely turned out of South Valley.

The Russians continued to hold part of the Causeway Heights, for General Liprandi with his infantry and field artillery still lingered around the sites of the captured redoubts up to and including No. 3: but the whole of General Ryjoff's defeated cavalry had moved to a position so far down North Valley as to be within a mile of the aqueduct running alongside the Tchernaya. Here, drawn up across North Valley, with their guns in front of them, they linked the Causeway force with General Jabrokritsky's troops on the Fedioukine Hills to the north of the valley. The Russians also had six squadrons of lancers under the command of Colonel Jeropkine: these were placed in two bodies of three squadrons each, the one in a fold of the Fedioukine Hills, and the other in a ravine on the side of the Causeway Heights, so as to be able to fall upon either flank of any allied troops which, 'in pressing Liprandi's retreat, might pursue it far down North Valley'. But North Valley itself, a thousand yards wide, was empty of troops, and the men holding the redoubts had little support. With this in mind the Russians began to remove the guns from the redoubts, with the idea of immobilizing the redoubts should they be retaken by the British.

Lord Raglan, watching from the edge of the Chersonese plateau, could see all these movements developing, and decided the time had come to retake the redoubts. The two divisions of infantry ordered down from the plateau two hours earlier should now have come into action; but although the 1st Division under the Duke of Cambridge was approaching, General Cathcart had delayed bringing down the 4th Division, and it was the 4th

145

General Liprandi

Division which had been chosen to recapture the redoubts.
Realizing the urgency, and not wanting to wait for the 4th
Division – or use the 1st, bearing in mind the big part they had
played at Alma – Lord Raglan made the fatal decision of ordering
his cavalry to do the job.

Lord Raglan thus proceeded to send a series of vague orders to
Lord Lucan to get the cavalry on the move, each of which Lord
Lucan misunderstood and misinterpreted. The first order[1] told
him 'to advance and take advantage of any opportunity to recover
the heights'. This appears straightforward, but it also added that

1. *There were two earlier orders to the infantry, so this is usually termed the third
order.*

he would be 'supported by the infantry', which Lucan wrongly interpreted as meaning he should wait for the infantry. Consequently he only moved the Light Brigade a little towards North Valley, where there was a better view of the enemy, and then waited for the infantry to arrive.

Lord Raglan looked down with growing impatience. William Russell of *The Times* saw him raise his telescope to his eye and lower it again with a gesture of frustration. Along the Causeway Heights there was activity. Through their glasses the watchers could make out teams of Russian artillery horses trailing lasso tackle. 'Look!' a staff officer called out. 'They're going to take away the guns.' But still Lord Lucan did not move. In desperation, Lord Raglan called for General Airey, his chief-of-staff, to send Lord Lucan another message. This, scribbled with additions at Lord Raglan's dictation on a flimsy sheet of paper supported on Airey's sabretache, told the cavalry 'to advance rapidly to the front to try to prevent the enemy carrying away the guns'. As General Airey's A.D.C. went off with the order, Lord Raglan called after him to tell Lord Lucan to attack immediately.

Captain Nolan of the 15th Hussars, General Airey's A.D.C., was a strange character. He had held a commission in the Austrian army, he had served in India, and he had written books on cavalry tactics. By his fellow officers he was considered something of a prig. 'A great man in his own estimation' was how Lord George described him. His contempt for both Cardigan and Lucan was violently and frequently expressed. The Noble Yachtsman and Lord Look-on were his names for them. Because of all this, he was not a very sound choice to take a message to either Lord Lucan or Lord Cardigan. However, he was a skilful horseman; and as the route down the cliffs to the cavalry below was a difficult one, he was a good man to deliver the message speedily. Captain Nolan went diving down the hill by the straightest and quickest route; and the watchers held their breath as they saw him slithering, scrambling and stumbling down to the plain. Arriving with his horse blowing and sweating, he handed over the creased and shabby-looking message to Lord Lucan who was sitting his horse between his two brigades. Lord Lucan read it slowly, with the customary deliberation which always infuriated his staff, and on this occasion caused Nolan to quiver with impatience. Then he muttered that it seemed a dangerous and probably useless operation to try and tackle artillery with cavalry alone. Captain Nolan was quite exasperated at hearing the man he hated challenging the commander-in-chief's order of which he was the bearer.

Lord Cardigan, the commander of the Light Brigade

Forgetting difference in rank, he shouted at Lord Lucan that Lord Raglan's orders were 'for the cavalry to attack immediately'. For such a tone to be used by a mere A.D.C. to a general was unheard of. Lord Lucan turned angrily on Nolan and said, 'Attack? Attack what? What guns?' Nolan threw back his head, and with even more lack of respect flung out his arm and pointed, not at the Causeway redoubts which the cavalry were supposed to try to retake in order to stop the Russians removing their guns, but to the end of North Valley where the Russian cavalry defeated by the Heavy Brigade had just established themselves behind the twelve guns of their horse artillery in battery. As he did so, he exclaimed, 'There, my lord, is your enemy; there are your guns.' Nolan was no doubt so angry by this time that he was not looking very carefully where he was pointing; but the result was the same as if he had meant to tell the cavalry to attack the far-off Russian horse artillery guns at the end of North Valley; and Lord Lucan shrugged his shoulders and trotted off to tell Lord Cardigan to do just this.

Lord Lucan found Lord Cardigan in front of the Light Brigade, and passed on the commander-in-chief's order. Coldly polite, Lord Cardigan brought down his sword in salute as acknowledgement.

'Certainly, sir!' he said in his loud, husky voice. 'But allow me to point out that the Russians have a battery in the valley in our front, and batteries and riflemen on each flank.'

'I know it,' replied Lord Lucan. 'But Lord Raglan will have it. We have no choice but to obey. Advance very steadily, and keep the men in hand.'

Lord Cardigan made no further comment. He saluted again, turned his horse, and murmuring to himself, 'Well, here goes the last of the Brudenells,' rode off to find Lord George Paget.

The Light Brigade had been halted near No. 6 Redoubt for over an hour. Most of the men had dismounted: some were eating biscuits and hard-boiled eggs; a few generous ones were sharing rum with their fellows: others had pulled out pipes. As soon as Lord Lucan was seen approaching, however, the order was given to mount. Colonel Shewell of the 8th Hussars, stern, pious and

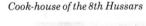

Cook-house of the 8th Hussars

not much liked, noticed a man with a pipe still in his mouth. Shouting that he was disgracing the regiment by smoking in the presence of the enemy, he ordered him to put it away. Out still farther in front, Lord George was enjoying a cigar, and he wondered whether he should put it out. Was it right for a senior officer to be smoking when Shewell was upbraiding a man for the same fault? However, Lord George was loth to throw away a good smoke. He kept it in his mouth, and it lasted until he reached the enemy's guns.

Lord Cardigan, meanwhile, rode up and told Lord George they had been ordered to advance to the front and attack the enemy. 'You will take command of the second line,' he added; 'and I expect your best support, mind, your best support.' This last sentence he repeated several times, and with too much force for Lord George's liking; but it caused him to answer with equal emphasis, 'Of course, my lord, you shall have my best support.'

Lord Cardigan then galloped off to the front of the brigade and drew it up: the 13th Light Dragoons under Captain Oldham on the right; the 17th Lancers, Lord Lucan's regiment, under Captain Morris on the left; the 11th Hussars, Lord Cardigan's regiment and under Colonel Douglas, at first were on the left of the 17th, but, on Lord Lucan's orders, moved back behind the front line; finally, in the rear under Lord George, were the 8th Hussars commanded by Colonel Shewell on the right, and his own regiment the 4th Light Dragoons on the left.

Private Wightman, who was present with the 17th Lancers, has given a stirring account of the charge. He saw Captain Nolan joining the brigade after delivering his fatal message. He noticed him having a momentary talk with Lord Cardigan, and then, presumably with his permission, falling in behind on the right of Captain Morris who had taken post in front of the 17th's left squadron.

In his strong hoarse voice Lord Cardigan called out: 'The Brigade will advance! First Squadron of the 17th Lancers direct!' 'Calm as on parade – calmer indeed than usual on parade – stately, square and erect, with his stern firm face and soldierly bearing, master of himself, his brigade and his charger, Lord Cardigan looked the ideal cavalry leader.' His long military seat in the saddle suited Ronald, the chestnut Wightman's father, his riding-master, had broken for him. He was in the full uniform of his old regiment the 11th Hussars; and he wore his pelisse, not slung, but put on like a patrol jacket, its front a blaze of gold lace.

Turning his head towards his trumpeter, Britten of the Lancers, he said quietly, 'Sound the Advance!' and wheeled his horse to face the dark mass at the farther end of the valley which they knew to be the enemy. The trumpeter sounded the 'Walk' and after a few horse-lengths came the 'Trot'. Wightman did not hear the 'Gallop'; but it was sounded. Neither voice nor trumpet, so far as he knew, ordered the 'Charge'; for Britten was a dead man in a few strides after he had sounded the 'Gallop'. They had ridden barely 200 yards, and were still at the trot, when Captain Nolan met his fate. He left his place to gallop forward and warn Lord Cardigan that he was going in the wrong direction; but Lord Cardigan considered his interference an impertinence, and paid no heed. Then a shell exploded near the front rank of the 17th, and a fragment struck Nolan through the heart. His sword arm remained upraised and rigid, his other limbs curled in on his contorted body as by a spasm, so that they wondered how the huddled form kept the saddle. A sudden convulsive twitch of the bridle hand inward on the chest caused the charger to wheel rearward abruptly; and then with a weird shriek – which annoyed Lord Cardigan still more because he believed Nolan was bawling impertinently – the horse and its gruesome rider disappeared.

As the line broke, at the trumpet sound, from the trot into the gallop, Lord Cardigan, almost directly in front of Wightman, turned his head leftwards towards Captain Morris and shouted hoarsely, 'Steady, steady, Captain Morris.' A squadron of the 17th Lancers had been named as directing squadron, and Morris as commander of the 17th was therefore responsible for both 'the pace and direction of the whole line'. Later, when they were in the midst of their torture, and mad to be out of it and have their revenge, and were forcing the pace, Lord Cardigan's sonorous command was heard again, 'Steady, steady the 17th Lancers!' and he checked with his outstretched sword Captain White who had shot abreast of him. But resolute man though he was, the time had come when neither his commands nor example could restrain the pace of his brigade; and when indeed to maintain his position in advance, if he were to escape being ridden down, he had to let his charger out from the gallop to the charge. For hell had opened upon them from front and either flank, and it kept open upon them during the minutes – they seemed hours – which passed while they traversed the mile and a quarter at the end of which were the enemy guns. The broken and fast-thinning ranks raised rugged peals of wild fierce cheering that only swelled the louder as the shot and shell from the flank batteries tore gaps through them, and the enfilading musketry fire from the infantry on both flanks

Charge of the Light Brigade

brought down horses and men. Yet in this stress it was fine to see how strong was the bond of discipline and obedience. 'Close in! close in!' was the constant command of the squadron and troop officers as the casualties made gaps in the ragged line, but the order was scarcely needed, for on their own initiative, and as it seemed mechanically, men and horses alike sought to regain touch.

Before they had broken into the charge, the right-hand man of the 17th, old John Lee, was all but smashed by a shell; he gave Wightman's arm a twitch, as with a strange smile he quietly said, 'Domino! chum,' and fell out of the saddle. His old grey mare kept alongside for some distance, treading on and tearing out her entrails as she galloped, till at length she dropped with a strange shriek. Peter Marsh was Wightman's left-hand man, and next beyond him was Private Dudley. The explosion of a shell had swept down four men on Dudley's left, and Wightman heard him ask Marsh if he had noticed what a hole 'that bloody shell had made' on his left front. 'Hold your foul-mouthed tongue,' answered Peter. 'Swearing like a blackguard when you may be knocked into eternity next minute!' Just then Wightman got a musket bullet through his right knee, and another in the shin, and his horse had three bullet wounds in the neck. Man and horse were

Private Wightman and the 17th Lancers

bleeding so fast that Marsh begged him to fall out. But he would not, pointing out that in a few minutes they must be into them. Instead, he sent his spurs well home and faced it out with his comrades. It was about this time that Sergeant Talbot had his head clean carried off by a round shot, yet for about thirty yards farther the headless body kept the saddle, the lance at the charge firmly gripped under the right arm.

They were nearly out of it at last, and close on those cursed guns. Lord Cardigan was still in front, steady as a church, but now his sword was in the air; he turned in his saddle for an instant and shouted his final command: 'Steady! Steady! Close in!' Immediately afterwards there crashed into them a regular volley from the Russian cannon. Wightman saw Captain White go down and Lord Cardigan disappear into the smoke. A moment more and he was in it himself. A shell burst over his head with a hellish crash that all but stunned him. Immediately afterwards he felt his horse take a tremendous leap into the air. What the horse jumped he never saw or knew; for the smoke was so thick he could not see his arm's length around him. Through the dense veil he heard noises of fighting and slaughter, but saw no obstacle, no adversary, no gun or gunner, and, in short, was through and beyond the Russian battery before he knew for certain that he had reached it.

He then found that none of his comrades was close to him, and there was no longer any semblance of a line. None of the lancers was on his right, but there was a group a little way on his left. Lord Cardigan must have increased his distance during or after passing through the battery, for he could now be seen some way ahead in the midst of a knot of Cossacks. At this moment Lieutenant Maxse, his lordship's A.D.C., came back out of the tussle badly wounded, and crossed Wightman's front. He called out, 'For God's sake, lancer, don't ride over me!' and pointing at Lord Cardigan, added, 'Rally on him!' Wightman was hurrying on towards the brigade commander, when a Cossack came at him and sent a lance into his right thigh. Wightman went for him, but he bolted. Then Wightman overtook him, drove a lance in his back and unhorsed him just in front of two Russian guns which were in possession of Sergeant-Majors Lincoln and Smith of the 13th Light Dragoons and other men of the brigade. When pursuing the Cossack, Wightman noticed Colonel Mayow, the brigade-major, deal very cleverly with a big Russian cavalry officer. He tipped his shako with the point of his sword, and then laid his head right open with the old cut seven. The chase of his Cossack

155

had diverted Wightman from rallying on Lord Cardigan. He was now nowhere to be seen, nor did Wightman ever see him again.

The handful with the guns to which he momentarily attached himself were presently outnumbered and overpowered. Troop Sergeant-Major Lincoln, however, escaped. He then rode towards Private Samuel Parkes[1] of the 4th Light Dragoons, who, supporting with one arm the wounded Trumpet-Major Crawford of his regiment, was with his other cutting and slashing at the enemy surrounding him; and Wightman struck in to help him until Parkes' sword was shot away and he was overwhelmed and captured. Then Wightman, with difficulty, cut his way out and joined Mustard of his own regiment and Fletcher of the 4th Light Dragoons. They were now through and on the farther side of a considerable body of the Russian cavalry, and so near the bottom of the valley that they could see quite clearly the Tchernaya river. But they were all three wearied and weakened by loss of blood, their horses were wounded in many places, there were enemy all about them, and they thought it about time to be getting back. Wightman remembered reading in the regimental library of an officer who said to his commander, 'We have done enough

1. Parkes was awarded the V.C., see Appendix A.

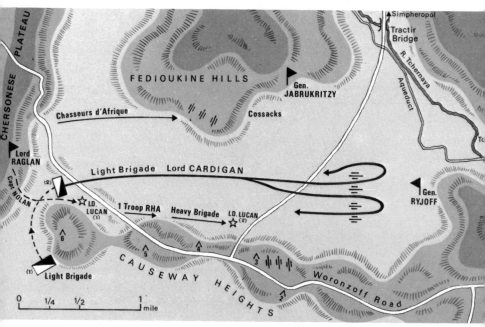

The Charge of the Light Brigade

156

for honour.' That was now his opinion, and they turned their horses' heads. They forced a way through ring after ring of enemy, fell in with Peter Marsh and rode rearward, breaking through party after party of Cossacks, until they heard the familiar voice of Corporal Morley[1] of their regiment, a great, rough, bellowing Nottingham man. He had lost his lance and hat, and his long hair was flying out in the wind as he roared, 'Coom 'ere! Coom 'ere! Fall in! lads, fall in!' With shouts and oaths, he collected some twenty troopers from various regiments. Wightman fell in with these men, among whom was Private John Penn of the 17th Lancers. Penn, a tough old warrior who had served with the 3rd Light Dragoons in the Sikh Wars, had killed a Russian officer, had dismounted, and with great deliberation accoutred himself with the belt and sword of the defunct, in which he made a great show – he was awarded the D.C.M. later.

A body of Russian Hussars now blocked the way. Morley, roaring Nottingham oaths by way of encouragement, led them straight at the Russians, and they went through and out the other side as though through tinsel paper. As they rode back up the valley, pursued by some Hussars and Cossacks, Wightman's horse was wounded by a bullet in the shoulder, and he was hard put to get the beast along. Presently they came abreast of some enemy infantry who fired into their right side; then came a similar series of volleys from more infantry on the left. Their firing was very impartial, for their own Hussars and Cossacks following close behind suffered too. Wightman's horse was now shot dead, riddled with bullets, and he too was shot in the forehead and top of the shoulder. Then while struggling out from under his dead horse, a Cossack standing over him stabbed him with a lance in the neck near the jugular, and again above the collar-bone, several times in the back, and once under the short rib; and when, having regained his feet, he was trying to draw his sword, a lance was pushed through the palm of his hand. This was the end. Fletcher at the same time lost his horse and was wounded, and both were made prisoner.

Not many of Corporal Morley's party got back, but a few did; and so did Lord George Paget and Lord Cardigan, and also several remnants of other regiments.

1. *Morley took his discharge in 1856 because he was not awarded the D.C.M., which certainly, according to Wightman, should have been given him. He went to America, fought on the Northern side all through the Civil War, was twice taken prisoner, spent a year in 'Libby' prison, retired with the rank of captain, and was later employed in the War Department at Washington.*

British Light Cavalry attacking the Russian guns at Balaclava

Lord George had pushed his 4th Light Dragoons well to the front in order to implement his promise to give Lord Cardigan his 'best support'; and it was the 17th Lancers and the 4th and 13th Light Dragoons who bore the brunt, the last being reduced to two officers and eight men. The 11th Hussars, who were in front of the 4th at the start and behind the 17th Lancers, edged off to the left and went round the line of Russian guns. They came up against a mass of Russian cavalry, and when their regiment turned back they were met by Lord George and some of the 4th. Reining in his horse, Lord George shouted, 'Halt front; if you don't front my boys we are done.' The 11th checked, and with admirable steadiness the whole group halted and fronted the oncoming Russian cavalry as if on parade. The movement had hardly been completed, however, when a formidable body of Russian lancers were seen blocking the retreat route back up the valley. Still Lord George did not lose heart. There seemed little hope; their horses were worn out and many men wounded, but he ordered them about again; and helter-skelter, jamming in spurs, they followed their gallant leader in a desperate charge at the lancers. Surprisingly, the Russians let them through just as the other group had Morley's men; and without further loss, they began the painful retreat back up the valley.

They had been preceded by Lord Cardigan. Beyond the guns, amid the smoke, he had been recognized by Prince Radziwill who put his Cossacks on to capturing alive the English nobleman he had once met in London. Lord Cardigan avoided that indignity. Considering it no part of a general's duty to fight among private soldiers, he took evasive action by losing himself in the smoke, and then left the fight, riding back slowly alone up the valley without being attacked further, and leaving his men to extricate themselves as best they could. To give him his due, there was so much smoke that he could not see them, nor they him. Several officers, including Colonel Mayow his brigade-major, were heard calling out, 'Where is Lord Cardigan?'

The 8th Hussars, restrained by the iron hand of their stern commander Colonel Shewell, had entered the fight last, but were

General Bosquet while watching the Charge exclaimed:
'C'est magnifique mais ce n'est pas la guerre!'

now fighting beyond the guns like the rest. Shewell too saw that he was cut off in the rear, and, wheeling his little force into line, charged at their head against the Russians blocking his path. Most of his men followed him successfully, and then the 8th began the painful trail home.

The Light Brigade carried through their charge largely unsupported. Captain Shakespear, realizing there were no targets clear of his own troops, halted I Troop soon after they had started down the valley. Lord Lucan did the same with the Heavy Brigade. Wearied by their earlier action, they followed the Light Brigade slowly and were left far behind. Then they came under crossfire from the Causeway Heights and Fedioukine Hills. Lord Lucan in the lead was wounded in the leg, and his horse was hit in two places; one of his A.D.C.s was killed and two of his staff wounded. Looking back, he saw that the two leading regiments were suffering casualties: in the Royals in front Colonel Yorke was severely wounded and twenty-one troopers were disabled. General Lucan

Chasseurs d'Afrique

160

I GORN.ᵗ MICHIEL. vii GORN.ᵗ CHAMBERLAIN xiii CAP.ⁿ JENYNS.
II CAP.ᵗⁿ GARDNER. viii P.ᵗᵉ MORRISEY. xiv SERG.ᵗ MULKAY.
III — — SMITH . ix V.SURG.ᵗ TOWERS. xv P.ᵗᵉ LONG
IV R.S.M. JOHNSON. x SERG.ᵗ MAHONEY. xvi T.S.M. LINGOLN.
V COL.ᵗ DOHERTY. xi T.S.M. HUNT. xvii P.ᵗᵉ GARDNER.
VI CORP.ᵗ GLYNN . xii P.ᵗᵉ DEARLOVE .

Remnant of the 13ᵗʰ Light Dragoons = Taken in front of their Camp, — on the morning after the — Charge of Balaclava. Octʳ 26ᵗʰ 1854.

had already taken over command from General Scarlett who had gone forward to reconnoitre. Deciding now that the only use to which the Heavy Brigade could be put was to protect the light cavalry against pursuit when they returned, and judging that for this they had come far enough, he ordered the halt to be sounded, and then retired the brigade out of range. As he did so he was heard to remark: 'They have sacrificed the Light Brigade; they shall not have the Heavy.'

The French meanwhile were more co-operative. They watched with distress the Light Brigade riding down the valley to their destruction, and, like Lord Raglan, could not understand why they did not turn against the redoubts, and why the Heavy Brigade did not join in. '*C'est magnifique, mais ce n'est pas la guerre,*' murmured General Bosquet in words which have been remembered ever since. '*Je suis vieux! j'ai vu des batailles; mais ceçi est trop,*' exclaimed another. However, they did more than lament. The 4th regiment of the Chasseurs d'Afrique under General d'Allonville, which had been waiting at the foot of the cliffs, charged over rough ground among tall undergrowth reaching to their girths through the Russian skirmishers on the

161

west of the Fedioukine Hills right up to the enemy guns which had been playing such havoc on the flank of the British cavalry. Before General Jabrokritsky could move up the Vladimir infantry in support, his artillery were forced to hook in and pull away; and on the return of the Light Brigade there was no crossfire from the west. All this at the expense of ten killed and twenty-eight wounded. A very gallant and worthwhile sacrifice by the French for their allies.

Meanwhile, while the bleeding remnants of the Light Brigade dragged themselves back to safety, some running, some limping, some crawling, and with fewer horses then men, and not many of either, Lord Cardigan rode up to one group of survivors and said in his loud hoarse voice by way of apology, 'It was a mad-brained trick; but it was no fault of mine.' To which they generously replied, 'Never mind, my lord; we are ready to go again.' Next he met Lord Raglan who angrily asked what he meant by charging a battery in front contrary to all the rules of cavalry tactics. 'My lord,' Cardigan replied, confident of his rectitude, 'I hope you will not blame me, for I received the order to attack from my superior officer in front of the troops.' With this Lord Raglan had to appear satisfied; and Lord Cardigan was able to ride back to his yacht with a clear conscience; but the commander-in-chief was not so forgiving to Lord Lucan. He told him that he had lost the Light Brigade by not using his discretion and stopping the charge. This Lord Lucan challenged forcibly, but found it difficult to convince anyone but himself.

THE 4ᵀᴴ DIVISION
AT BALACLAVA

✶

THE 4ᵀᴴ DIVISION
AT BALACLAVA

*'It is impossible that there can be one as far away as
that. It is the most extraordinary thing I ever saw, for
the position is more extensive than that occupied by
the Duke of Wellington at Waterloo.'*

GENERAL SIR GEORGE CATHCART
ON BEING POINTED OUT THE REDOUBT
ON CANROBERT'S HILL

Captain Ewart's account of the Battle of Balaclava explains why
the 4th Division was so tardy, and why it did not take an active
part until the charge of the Light Brigade was over.

Early on the morning of 25 October, a messenger arrived at
headquarters bringing news of the Russian attack on the Balaclava position. Lord Raglan and the staff were soon mounted, and
rode off to the cliff edge near the Col. The Col was the name
given to the place where the direct road from Balaclava and
Kadikoi climbed up on to the Chersonese plateau – there being an
isolated hill nearby. The other way up was by the Woronzoff road
farther north. On reaching the Col, they could see shells bursting
over the redoubts occupied by the Turks, and almost immediately
afterwards, the retreat of the Turks in the utmost confusion
towards Kadikoi. Seeing this, Lord Raglan sent Ewart with a
message to General Sir George Cathcart asking him to move the
4th Division down to the plain to help Sir Colin Campbell in the
defence of Balaclava. He was just starting with the order, when
General Airey came up and said, 'Remember you are on no account
to let the division use the Woronzoff road.' Ewart galloped off as
hard as he could go, and on reaching the camp of the 4th Division
found Sir George dressed and seated in a chair in his tent. He at
once delivered the message, upon which the general replied, 'It is
quite impossible for the 4th Division to move.' Ewart then said his
orders were very positive, and that the Russians were advancing
on Balaclava. Sir George replied, 'I cannot help that; my division
cannot move, for the greater portion of the men have only just

165

come up from the trenches before Sebastopol.' For the third time Ewart repeated his orders, stating that he had seen for himself the Turks fleeing from the redoubts towards Balaclava, and that every moment was of consequence, as Sir Colin had only got the 93rd to depend on besides the cavalry. Sir George then said, 'Well, you may return to Lord Raglan, and tell him that I cannot move my division.'

Ewart saluted, and rode off a few yards from the tent to consider how it would be best for him to act under the circumstances. After a few minutes' thought he came to the conclusion that to return to Lord Raglan would be downright folly as he would doubtless have left the Col, and would take a long time to locate; and the 93rd Highlanders alone, except for the cavalry, were insufficient to defend Balaclava unless support reached them soon. Never before had he been placed in so painful and embarrassing a position. However, his mind was soon made up. Although he felt sure that the 93rd would fight as long as a man was left alive, he was determined to make one more effort to obtain help for his regiment. He returned to Sir George, and stated firmly, but most respectfully, that he would not return to Lord Raglan, that he had been sent for the 4th Division, and that he would remain until it was made ready, that much valuable time had already been lost, that matters were probably in a critical state at Balaclava, and that he still hoped the division would be turned out. Sir George listened very attentively to all he urged, and at last, to his great relief, said, 'Very well, I will consult with my staff officers and see if anything can be done.' The general then went away, and after a short time, to Ewart's great joy, he heard the bugles sounding, and soon saw the division begin to fall in.

Ewart told Sir George that General Airey had said the division was on no account to march by the Woronzoff road, so they started in the direction of the Col which was the only other route; for although infantry on its own could have gone direct to Kadikoi by going down the cliffs on to the plain of South Valley, the way was steep and covered with brushwood, and the artillery of the division would have had to go by the Col road; in fact, it was by far the best way for the 4th Division to move to the assistance of Sir Colin at Balaclava, which was the original order Ewart had taken to Sir George from Lord Raglan. But by coming down into South Valley after the 93rd's stand and the Heavies' charge, which cleared the Russian cavalry out of South Valley and sent them back over the Causeway, the 4th Division did not see the battle going on in North Valley and they began to occupy the nearest redoubts in ignorance of what was occurring on the other side of the Causeway Heights. However, General Airey's instructions not to move by the Woronzoff road were most proper ones at the time, as by that road the division would have had to move in column in fours, thereby causing delay, and would also have been liable, after descending to the plain, to be cut off or fired at before reaching Balaclava, their original destination; whereas by taking the other road they were out of Russian range and supported by allied batteries on the plateau and the Marine Heights.

On descending by the Col, the division went to the right of the vineyard and cavalry camps, and was making for Balaclava when a staff officer galloped up to them and called out, 'You are going the wrong way.' General Airey then appeared, and said to Cathcart, 'Lord Raglan wishes you to advance immediately and recapture the redoubts from the Russians.' This order was given very plainly and then General Airey turned to Ewart and said, 'Captain Ewart, you know the position of the redoubts; stay with Sir George and show him where they are.'

Later, Sir George asked Ewart to point them out, and on his doing so, at once said, 'You must be mistaken.' Ewart replied that he had made no mistake, and pointed them out again. When he was indicating the position of No. 1 Redoubt on Canrobert's Hill, Sir George muttered, 'It is impossible that there can be one as far away as that.' Ewart patiently explained that he had surveyed them all on the ground, and been inside No. 1; and then Sir George observed, 'Well, it is the most extraordinary thing I ever saw, for the position is more extensive than that occupied by the Duke of Wellington's army at Waterloo' (at which battle he had been present).

Some French troops had by this time come down on to the plain, and the Guards and the 42nd and 79th Highlanders were descending a narrow path down the cliffs bordering the plateau; so Sir George turned his division back and led it between the cliffs and the vineyard towards the rear of No. 6 Redoubt, in the direction of the other supporting troops. No. 6 Redoubt was found empty, and Sir George at first ordered some of the Rifle Brigade to man it. He changed his mind, however, saying, 'No, I shall want the Rifles to skirmish ahead; put some men of a red regiment in.' Then they moved on to No. 5 Redoubt where some more men were left, and so on to No. 4. Here they first came under enemy fire and round shot began to fly past them, and many riderless horses galloped by, some apparently belonging to the Greys. They found No. 4 Redoubt deserted, and the guns dismounted and spiked; and Sir

George now deployed his division in two lines and ordered his men to lie down while P Battery opened fire on No. 3 Redoubt ahead which was still occupied by the Russians. Several rounds were fired, and the Russians replied, but the range was too great for much effect. The 1st Battalion of the Rifle Brigade under Colonel Horsford was then sent forward to skirmish towards the redoubt, and soon afterwards the Russians withdrew, and fire from No. 3 ceased.

Ewart now went up to the north side of the Causeway, and just as he did so, a party of horsemen rode by at full speed, one of whom called out, 'We have just passed a staff officer lying badly wounded.' At that time Ewart was not able to leave Sir George, and could do nothing to help. Soon afterwards Lord Cardigan rode past. He called out, saying that he had lost the whole of his brigade, and pointed to a hole in his overalls where a Cossack had stuck a lance. The cavalry had been in the valley on the other side of the ridge of the Causeway; but the 4th Division had seen nothing of them until now, and had no idea another charge had been made.

Released by Sir George, Ewart crossed over the ridge of the Causeway, and galloped down the North Valley a little way towards the enemy. At no very great distance, he found poor Nolan with a dreadful wound in his chest, quite dead; and a few yards farther on he came upon Captain Morris, who had been a fellow staff officer at headquarters until he left to command the 17th Lancers. Ewart dismounted and spoke to him; but he was almost insensible. There was a terrible wound in his head and another in one of his arms. A little farther on was a man from the Heavies with his jaw frightfully smashed. Ewart asked him his regiment, but he could not speak, and only pointed to his buttons, from which Ewart saw he belonged to the 5th Dragoon Guards. As he could not lift Morris or the others by himself, Ewart rode back to No. 4 Redoubt. Finding the Turks had returned, he made signs that he urgently wanted assistance, and persuaded about half a dozen to accompany him back down the valley. On reaching Nolan's body, he got two of them to lift it, and then went on with the others to Morris and the dragoon; but just at that moment the Russians opened fire, and one or two round shot whizzed by. In an instant poor Nolan was dropped, and away ran all the Turks back to No. 4 Redoubt. Ewart could do nothing alone, so again went for help, and seeing a trooper on horseback begged him to go as hard as he could to the 17th Lancers and tell them their commanding officer was lying badly wounded out in front, and that

168

Duke of Cambridge

some stretchers ought to be sent at once. The man promised to go immediately, and Ewart returned to the 4th Division which had remained on the south side of the ridge. Some little time afterwards, one or two stretchers appeared, and Morris, the dragoon and Nolan were brought in – the Russians again firing. The last time Ewart saw Morris, he was having his wounds dressed by a surgeon, James Mouat, on the side of the hill near No. 4 Redoubt. The body of Nolan was buried the same afternoon in the ditch of No. 5 Redoubt. Ewart heard later that both Morris and the dragoon recovered.

The Duke of Cambridge now came forward to see Sir George, and Sir Colin Campbell rode across from Kadikoi and joined them. Having pulled back the Rifles, the three generals went forward up to No. 4 Redoubt to view the position. The Russians, seeing so

169

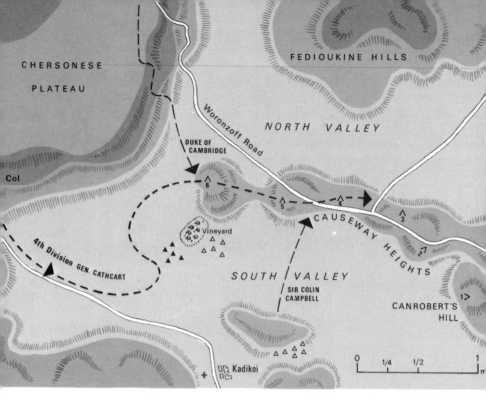

CHERSONESE
PLATEAU

FEDIOUKINE HILLS

Woronzoff Road

NORTH VALLEY

DUKE OF
CAMBRIDGE

Col

6

5

4

3

2

1

CAUSEWAY HEIGHTS

Vineyard

4th Division GEN. CATHCART

SOUTH VALLEY

SIR COLIN
CAMPBELL

CANROBERT'S
HILL

Kadikoi

0   1/4   1/2   1
m

The 4th Division at Balaclava

many staff officers together, opened fire; and a cannon-ball passed
close to Ewart and took some of the feathers out of the cocked-
hat of one of the Duke's A.D.C.s.

The conference over, Ewart asked Sir George whether they had
decided to retake the redoubts still held by the enemy. Sir George
replied that they were not going to do so as it would be too costly
in lives; and he was about to send a message to that effect back to
Lord Raglan for his approval.

No further advance was now made, nor did the Russians attempt
any forward movements; both sides in fact seemed to think
enough had been done, and the battle ended. The Guards and 4th
Division returned to their lines before Sebastopol; the remnants
of the Light Brigade went up on to the plateau to a new camp by
the Windmill; the Heavies stayed down on the plain; and the 42nd
and 79th Highlanders were left with Sir Colin to assist in the
defence of Balaclava.

The Battle of Balaclava brought advantages for the British: it
safeguarded the direct route by the Col to Sebastopol and saved
Balaclava harbour; but the failure to follow up and retake all the
170

redoubts, and secure the use of the Woronzoff road, added later to the miseries of the British encamped on the plateau and in the trenches before Sebastopol. The direct road up via Kadikoi and the Col sufficed during the fine weather of the autumn, but it became well nigh impassable for periods in the winter which followed because of mud. Later a railway was built from the docks at Balaclava up to the Col; but until this was completed, the loss of the use of an additional road up on to the plateau from the harbour was a serious handicap to the administrative services; and this goes some way to explain the misery of the British in their first winter in the Crimea.

The Crimean War was one of the first of the modern wars as regards artillery, and massive indeed were its artillery bombardments from 8-inch howitzers, large mortars, 32-pounders, 24-pounders and other heavy guns on both sides; but in the battle of Balaclava the big guns were scarcely used. Lieutenant Roberts's battery and Lieutenant Wolfe's battery, and others on the heights near the harbour, did take part at times: and some of their shells 'burst beautifully close to the centre of the Russian column'; but usually they were out of range. The 6-pounders and 9-pounders of the horse and field artillery provided most support. On the morning of 25 October I Troop helped to hold off the Russians attacking the redoubts by coming into action on the right of No. 3 Redoubt; and W Battery came up from Kadikoi to support I Troop on the ridge; and then dropped back by half sections covering the retreat of the cavalry. Before and after the Heavies' charge, a few shells were dropped into the Russian columns by W Battery from their position at Kadikoi and from I Troop with the Light Brigade; but that was about all. During the charge of the Light Brigade, the artillery was employed hardly at all. However, from ammunition returns: C Troop and E Battery, officially attached to the Light Division, fired 34 rounds and 199 rounds respectively; F Battery, attached to the 3rd Division, 23 rounds; and P Battery, attached to the 4th Division, 166 rounds. The rounds from P are known to have been fired during the period of the Light Brigade charge, and some of the others may have been discharged at the same time. Some of the French guns on the edge of the plateau also came into action; but the Russians were out of their range for most of the battle.

The British cavalry fought well at Balaclava which was indeed essentially a cavalry battle. General Scarlett reacted quickly to the presence of the Russian cavalry on his flank, and his part in the charge of the Heavies was above criticism. Even a

171

hundred years ago it was considered that a general should not charge at the head of troops; but with Lord Lucan present – and always ready to take over, as in North Valley later – Scarlett was quite justified in leading his men into the fight. All the regiments of the Heavy Brigade charged fearlessly, and fought hard and skilfully; but the 4th Dragoon Guards gained most renown by entering the west flank of the Russian columns and fighting their way right through to the other side. As has been mentioned, the failure to pursue prevented complete success; but the Heavies had done all they could for the time being, and the Light Brigade had orders to remain where they were.

The Light Brigade's own charge was less effective, and the losses of 247 men killed and wounded and 475 horses killed of the 670 who made the charge were grievous. However, the net result of all the actions near Balaclava was that the Russian attack on the allied flank was thwarted for the time being.

It has been customary to sneer at Lord Lucan and Lord Cardigan in the manner of Captain Nolan and others who wrote, 'We all agree that two greater muffs than Lucan and Cardigan could not be; we call Lucan the cautious ass and Cardigan the dangerous ass; Lord Cardigan has as much brains as his boot and is only to be equalled in want of intellect by his relation the Earl of Lucan; without mincing matters, two such fools to take command could hardly be picked out of the British army; but then they are Earls!'

It is always a pleasure to hit out at the Establishment as these young men were doing; but a study of eye-witness accounts paints a different picture from theirs. Although he was generally unpopular, many officers respected Lord Lucan's efficiency and attention to detail, including the sensible Lord George Paget; and even Lord Cardigan was not without his admirers. The 11th Hussars were perfectly drilled and equipped when he was in command; and during the charge, Private Wightman of the 17th Lancers described him as 'the ideal cavalry leader' and said his long military seat admirably suited Ronald, the chestnut his father had broken for him. Then after his return from the charge, a group of men were heard to say, 'Never mind, my lord. We are ready to go again.' All of which suggests that the noble lords were not quite as useless as they are made out to be.

The Battle of Balaclava is usually described with the emphasis on the tragic charge of the Light Brigade. Here more weight has been given to the Heavy Brigade, the Artillery and the 93rd Highlanders, the only infantry regiment present until the end when the 4th Division arrived. The 93rd deserved the fame they won in the battle, as does Sir Colin Campbell who led them during the repulse of the charge of the Russian cavalrymen. In fact, Sir Colin conducted the defence of Balaclava most skilfully. He was ubiquitous: he was with Lord Lucan at No. 1 Redoubt in the early morning; he visited Lieutenant Roberts on the Marine Heights; he took command of 'The Thin Red Line' at Kadikoi, and visited the Heavies after their charge to congratulate the Greys. Finally he went over at No. 4 Redoubt to confer with Sir George Cathcart and the Duke of Cambridge at the end of the battle.

INKERMAN

INKERMAN

'General Pennefather's maxim was "whenever you see a head, hit it", and this was exactly what he tried to make the reinforcements do as they dribbled up to him, and they acted on his instructions to the letter; when they ran out of ammunition, they even hurled stones at the oncoming Russians' heads.'

In November, the British on the exposed eastern flank were again attacked by the Russian field army, this time in co-operation with a force making a sortie from Sebastopol. After a trial attack which is sometimes called Little Inkerman, and was easily repulsed, the main assault took place on the foggy morning of 5 November 1854. That day it was Captain Ewart's turn to ride round the divisions and find out the happenings of the previous night. He started from headquarters about 4 a.m., and rode first to the camp of the 3rd Division, visiting afterwards in succession those of the 4th, Light and 1st Divisions, and finally arriving at the 2nd Division on the extreme right in the area known as Inkerman from the ruins of Inkerman on the opposite side of the Tchernaya. Day was breaking as he reached the 2nd, and everything was still, the only signs of life being the horses and men belonging to the two guns which stood ready close to the tents on the road leading through the camp. He rode, as was customary, to the tent of one of the staff officers belonging to the division, and asked if there was anything to report to headquarters. The reply was 'Nothing whatever', and that it had been a 'particularly quiet night'. After wishing him good morning, it occurred to Captain Ewart that it might be better before returning to visit the old telegraph station at the top of the Woronzoff road from which an extensive view could be had; as he thought it more than probable that another attack would be made on Balaclava soon. He accordingly rode there and tried to discover whether the Russians near Tchorgoun were on the move. He had his field-glasses, but a thick mist hung over the Tchernaya, and he could see nothing. He was still gazing intently in the hope that the mist might clear when suddenly a few shots were fired in the direction of the 2nd Division picquets and the

177

Guards' picquet to their left, almost immediately followed by others in quick succession. He was near some French troops, and when he asked, 'What can the firing mean over there?' received the reply, 'Depend upon it, you are being attacked again!' Coming to the same conclusion, Ewart galloped off as hard as he could towards the firing. On his way he came upon Sir George Brown whose Light Division was in the process of turning out of their camp which lay just to the south-west of the 2nd Division's and west of the Guards'. He told Ewart to ride off at once and warn Lord Raglan; and on Ewart asking if he could go forward first and see what was happening, the general replied, 'No; don't lose a moment. Lord Raglan must be told immediately that we are being attacked.' The firing now had become very heavy, and, putting spurs to his horse, he quickly reached headquarters and made his report to General Airey. Lord Raglan was soon in the saddle, and in a few minutes they were all galloping towards Inkerman.

On their way, an officer was sent to warn the 4th Division whose camp was to the west of the Light; but he found that on the first alarum Sir George Cathcart had led his men over towards the Sandbag Battery, which he later tried to envelop by a turning movement round on the slope of the cliffs. The three Highland Regiments were guarding Balaclava; but Guards' picquets held the high spur jutting out into the Careening Ravine, and also the Sandbag Battery, so the Duke of Cambridge moved the rest of the Guards forward as well. When he asked Captain Paynter who was firing his guns into the mist, where the enemy were, Captain Paynter replied, 'They are all around us, but the thickest there,' pointing to the right front of the British position.

Prince Mentschikoff was at Sebastopol, and, with the sons of the Tsar, the Grand Dukes Nicholas and Michael, watched the battle from the rear; but General Dannenberg commanded the Russian attacking army with Generals Soimonoff and Pauloff under him in command of separate corps. During the night of 4 November, Soimonoff was to lead his troops quietly out of Sebastopol, while Pauloff's field army crossed the causeway and Inkerman Bridge over the Tchernaya at the head of the harbour. Meanwhile, Prince Gortschakoff with General Liprandi as his subordinate was to occupy the attention of the French under Bosquet in the rear of the British camps by threatening Balaclava and the cliffs at the eastern edge of the Chersonese plateau. It was a sound enough plan, but in the event did not work out well. The front which included the Careening and Quarry ravines was too narrow for two army corps even if Soimonoff had kept to the west

178

Sergeant Glasgow of the Royal Artillery

on the Victoria Ridge as was intended. When he led his troops instead over to the Careening Ravine, he pressed against Pauloff's men, with the result that the two corps got mixed up and were put into confusion. Also Prince Gortschakoff was not energetic enough in his feint attack to stop General Bosquet going to the aid of his allies.

When Lord Raglan and his staff arrived upon the scene, the battle was raging furiously. The Sandbag Battery, having no guns and occupied only by a Guards' picquet of forty men, was overrun by the Russians, but it was subsequently retaken by the 41st Regiment, and then changed hands several times. In fact, a feature of the fighting on the British right was this obsession by both sides with the Sandbag Battery which was really fairly useless as an entrenchment and not worth the effort taken to gain command of it.

Lord Raglan, according to Ewart, felt that he could personally do little or nothing because the mist stopped him seeing what was happening. Thus there was little higher direction, and Inkerman came to be called by the British 'The Soldiers' Battle'. All Lord Raglan and his staff did was to ride quietly about under a shower of shot and shell. One of the latter which burst in the midst of them mortally wounded General Strangways. When that poor old general who commanded the whole of the artillery was struck, he merely observed in a quiet tone, 'Will someone kindly assist me off my horse?' and then realizing that he was mortally wounded, added, 'Please take me away to die among my gunners.'

The Russians attacked in masses supported by tremendous artillery fire, and the task of the British was to prevent them overrunning the defences around the 2nd Division camp, a difficult task, as there were 40,000 Russians, with 100 guns on Shell Hill between the main ravines, against 8,000 British. The 2nd Division who bore the brunt was commanded by General Pennefather owing to Sir George de Lacy Evans being thrown from his horse and injured a few days earlier. Pennefather's maxim for fighting the battle was 'whenever you see a head, hit it', and this was exactly what he tried to make the reinforcements do as they dribbled up to him, and they acted on his instructions to the letter. When they ran out of ammunition, they even hurled stones at the oncoming Russians' heads.

The left and centre of the British front were stabilized first. The Guards' picquet at the head of Careening Ravine held fast, as did the Barrier at the head of Quarry Ravine in the centre; in both these areas, attack and counter-attack finally went in favour of the British. Captain Ewart says, 'It is invidious to single out any regiment or individual in a great battle like Inkerman where all fought well and did their best;' but the chronicles of the battle record that on the left and centre, besides the Guards, the 21st, 30th, the 47th, 49th, 50th, 57th, 63rd, 77th and 88th were among those who were outstanding; while for the artillery, G Battery, and Company Colour Sergeant Andrew Henry[1] won everlasting fame.

Although the Russians were held on the British left and centre, the right remained most insecure. The Sandbag Battery here changed hands time and time again; and the attempt by General Cathcart to envelop it by going half-way down the cliffs only

1. Henry was awarded the V.C.

resulted in his being killed by a musket-ball and his troops being decimated. Finally, however, two fortunate interventions turned the tide of battle in the favour of the British. First, some 18-pounders, which Lord Raglan had sent for, came into action on Home Ridge and got the better of the Russian guns on Shell Hill; and next, General Bosquet, having realized that Prince Gortschakoff had no serious intention of either attacking Balaclava or the cliffs, sent some of his regiments to help his allies. The first of these were two battalions of Zouaves, one being *les tirailleurs algériens* under colonel de Wimpffen who in his *notes et correspondance* tells of the part he played in the battle. He says:

We have just taken part in a sharp encounter in which my riflemen did brilliantly. The English were taken by surprise just as their dawn *réveillé* was being sounded. Several of their

General Cathcart's death at the Battle of Inkerman

badly defended posts were overrun [only the Sandbag Battery, in fact] and the enemy was in among their tents while they were still tumbling out of them alarmed by the noise. Across the North Valley of Balaclava Russian cavalry supported by artillery were menacing the French defence line along the edge of the cliffs and firing at us although they were too far away to do much harm. General Bosquet saw that this was only a decoy to stop us going to the help of our allies, and sent forward General Bourbaki's brigade without regard to it . . . *Mais les Anglais, par un faux sentiment d'amour propre refusaient nos services.*

Later, however, they thought better of it, and sought French aid, and the French formations named above, including one of colonel de Wimpffen's battalions, advanced to help their allies.

Wimpffen's tirailleurs were moving forward with fixed bayonets when they were met by an excited English officer who called out to them, please, to hurry.

'*Je ne puis, Monsieur, aller avec plus de rapidité sans avoir à redouter un désordre ne me permettant point d'attaquer l'ennemi avec ensemble,*' replied colonel de Wimpffen sternly.

On this the English officer rode off back towards the front, only to re-appear, almost immediately, crying out:

'Bourbaki's brigade has been struck in the flank and is being overwhelmed.'

This *cri de coeur* had more effect on Colonel Wimpffen. Gathering his Zouaves around him, he pointed at the Sandbag Battery and gave them the order to charge. Thus, to cries of 'Allah! Allah!' with six enormous negroes in the van, the tirailleurs, eyes rolling and uttering heart-tearing yells, hurled themselves on the Russians guarding the battery. Then, just as they had got under way, the impetus of the charge was halted. Buglers were heard on the flanks sounding the retreat; and simultaneously colonel de Wimpffen's horse was struck in the chest and dropped in its tracks breaking the colonel's scabbard in its fall and hurling him to the ground. One of his men, however, took the saddle and pistols from the dead horse lest they should fall into the hands of the enemy, and Captain Gibon gave his horse to the colonel. Then the charge was begun again, and although a shell burst near him and wounded his new mount slightly he was able to ride into the battery unscathed surrounded by his tirailleurs, and driving out the Russians before them. The tall Africans who, according to custom, had been his flank guards in the assault now gathered

182

round their colonel to find out whether he had been wounded by the hail of shot and shell which had assailed them during the charge; and they were astonished and delighted to find him unharmed.

'*Tu es un marabout, Dieu te protège,*' they exclaimed.

'*Oui, mes enfants,*' colonel de Wimpffen replied. '*Je suis marabout, parceque je vous aime.*'

Then one of the negroes went up to his colonel and kissed his hand saying that God being willing, he hoped it would always be so.

From the Russian side, Captain Hodasevich's account tallies well with the British and French accounts related above. Early in November 1854, he says, the Taroutine Regiment embarked from Fort Nicholas in steamers to go across to the north side of the harbour. They had been told they were to join a force which was to make a feint attack on Balaclava and the cliffs of the Chersonese plateau. They marched via the Mackenzie Heights and then moved south to Tchorgoun. At 11 a.m. on 2 November they crossed the Tchernaya and took up a position on Canrobert's Hill which had remained in Russian hands after the Battle of Balaclava. It was said that they would soon be attacking the allied position on the hills east of Balaclava to render the port useless. It was also said that they were only waiting for the arrival of Grand Dukes Nicholas and Michael.

However, there was a change of plan. First they were moved up to the Tractir Bridge and then farther north back to the area of the Belbec, north of Sebastopol. They arrived on the Belbec about 2.30 on the morning of 4 November, in a bad humour, for they felt that Prince Mentschikoff did not know what to do with their regiment, and had kept them continually on the move. On the Belbec they received an order from the Prince's staff to prepare 400 gabions and 200 fascines which were to be carried to the posthouse at Inkerman. As their regiment had never before made either gabions or fascines, officers who had been to cadet schools or served in the sappers were detailed to act as instructors. Captain Hodasevich was one of those detailed for this duty, and they did not finish their work until 8 p.m. Then a rumour amounting almost to a certainty became current that they were to attack the allies, but when, and on which side, no one knew. Preparations for battle, however, were visible everywhere: equipment being checked, pouches examined and stretchers taken out of the wagons.

During the evening they heard that the Grand Dukes Nicholas and Michael had arrived at last: Hodasevich's sergeant indeed assured him that he had seen them both himself. About 3 on the morning of 5 November the men were ordered to stand to their arms, each having previously received one glass of vodka. Then they began to move off in the direction of Sebastopol, but no one knew exactly where they were going; they only knew they were advancing against the allied army.

When they reached the Inkerman posthouse, they turned off along the causeway towards Inkerman bridge. Here they ran into General Dannenberg who with his large staff almost blocked the road. Hodasevich was able to find out from one of the General's A.D.C.s that there was to be a double attack: General Soimonoff's corps from Sebastopol was to advance up Victoria Ridge towards the Lancaster Battery, and Pauloff's corps, which included the Taroutine Regiment, was to advance towards Shell Hill, the Barrier, the Sandbag Battery and the windmill. The Taroutine Regiment was to lead over the bridge and the battalions behind them were to carry the fascines to revet battery positions for a hundred guns on Shell Hill. Hodasevich records that he estimated the total Russian force engaged in the attack at 40,000 men.

After a halt of about half an hour they began to move down towards the Tchernaya. They advanced in silence and in perfect order, although they never for a moment imagined that the allies would let them reach the bridge by the long causeway that led to it without trying to stop them. A couple of field-pieces on the road above the bridge could have swept it from end to end. In the event they reached the bridge unharmed. It has been hurriedly reconstructed during the night by sailors, and they asked them if they had seen the enemy. The sailors replied that the English were either asleep or busy making coffee in their entrenchments as they had been all round the hills and seen no one. Then they all began to consider their success as certain, for it was evident that the allies were going to be caught unawares.

Having crossed the bridge, they moved off to the right and began to ascend Shell Hill; but still neither shot nor shell was heard from either side. The day now began to break; but they were enveloped in a thick fog that the sun's rays could not penetrate, and they could only see a few paces ahead. In the queer foggy light of dawn the faces of the Russian soldiers looked ghostly pale so that Captain Hodasevich called out to Captain Vasmet: 'How pale you are!'

184

'Well, look at yourself!' Vasmet replied. And when Hodasevich pulled out of his pocket a small hairbrush with a looking-glass at the back, and ventured to take a peep at his own face, he found that like the rest of them he was as pale as a sheet.

Suddenly there was a shout 'To the left!' The Ekatherinenburg Regiment from the Sebastopol column were moving across the front, and the Taroutine Regiment had to conform and move left too; but in spite of this, the two columns began to get mixed up and confused, for the front had now become very narrow.

The Taroutine Regiment on moving to the left were brought over into Quarry Ravine; and as the descent was steep, their ranks became broken, and some men began to drop their knapsacks and relieve themselves of encumbrances like greatcoats and sapping tools. By dint of great exertion, Hodasevich managed to keep his company together and stopped most of his men from abandoning their kit. The ascent from the head of Quarry Ravine was more difficult than the descent had been; and it was so steep that they had to drag themselves up by catching hold of the brushwood.

When they emerged they saw men from other battalions in front of a small entrenchment (the Sandbag Battery) and these waved for them to join them. In the distance bugles could be heard sounding the advance, and several of Hodasevich's company broke ranks and started to run. When he restrained them and called them back, they cried out that the battle would be over before they got there. Pressing in on the entrenchment was a mixture of regiments: over on the right the Borodinos who were brigaded with the Taroutines under Pauloff were just coming out of Quarry Ravine; and behind were Soimonoff's Ekatherinenburgers busy helping themselves to the contents of the dropped knapsacks.

Hodasevich had just brought his company forward up into line with the other soldiers about forty yards from the battery emplacement, when looking back towards the harbour where the mist had cleared he noticed the Grand Dukes with Prince Mentschikoff watching the battle near the lower lighthouse.

'Look!' he called to his men. 'Over there by the lighthouse are the Grand Dukes. Mind you don't disgrace yourselves while they are watching you.' Every head turned; and in answer to a further call from Hodasevich of 'Do you see them?' they yelled back determinedly, 'We do, sir! We do!'

'Then, forward with the bayonet,' cried their leader; and with a loud shout the 120 men of his company stormed the battery, carrying with them the stragglers around.

As Hodasevich scrambled up the barbette of the battery, he saw a number of red-coated Englishmen in tall black hats making their way out of the back, who later he learnt were English Guards. These retreated about 400 yards and then turned and opened fire with their rifles on the Russians; then when some of them ran out of ammunition, they came nearer, and started throwing stones, one of which struck Hodasevich on the left shoulder. The battery was constructed to emplace two guns; but inside were only some kettles boiling on a fire for the breakfast the Guards had been preparing when the Russians attacked them.

Close by stood a young ensign named Protopopoff; and seeing that he looked glum, Hodasevich asked what was the matter.

'Ah!' he said. 'Tell my uncle to write home and say I was killed at the Battle of Inkerman' – his uncle was in Hodasevich's company.

Hodasevich said he ought not to joke like that; for didn't he see the day was theirs? But he had hardly time to pronounce the words before the ensign was struck in the back by a bullet and dropped dead.

Although the Russians had easily turned the Guards picquet out of the battery, once having gained possession, they made no effort to push on any farther. Indeed, there was considerable confusion in the neighbourhood of the battery from then on. The Ekatherinenburgers in the rear shot and killed one of Hodasevich's men; and the Tomsk Regiment shot up the Boutirsk Regiment, mistaking them for French from the shape of their caps which, although higher, resembled képis in the fog. The confusion was aggravated by the death of General Soimonoff early in the battle; but it was the mixing up of the two columns on too narrow a front combined with the difficulties of finding landmarks in the fog which was mostly to blame.

About 9.30 a.m., when the allies were seen to be advancing on the battery in force, a Russian bugler was heard sounding 'To the left about'; and this was too much for the disordered Russians. In spite of frantic cries from officers trying to stop them, they turned *en masse* and ran helter-skelter down the hill towards the river in the rear.

Here General Kiriakoff, commander of the 17th Division to which the Taroutines and Borodinos belonged, also tried to stop the flood of retreat.

'Halt, halt!' he yelled, frantically waving his Cossack whip, getting a few cuts at the men where he could, and berating the

186

officers for letting them get out of hand. It was to no avail, however. Although they shook themselves into some sort of order, they still made off towards the rear. Hodasevich records that some English prisoners being conducted back showed by the expression on their faces great surprise at such extraordinary behaviour by a Russian general.

Behind the rocks to the east of Quarry Ravine and beside Inkerman Bridge the scattered Russians finally consolidated; and the 11th Division moved back a little and formed a rearguard to protect the main body from any allied pursuit. While the companies were being mustered, the men regained their spirits sufficiently to show each other their plunder: one had found in the battery a revolver with one charge in the chamber but the cap gone – perhaps that one charge missing fire had cost the owner his

Battle of Inkerman

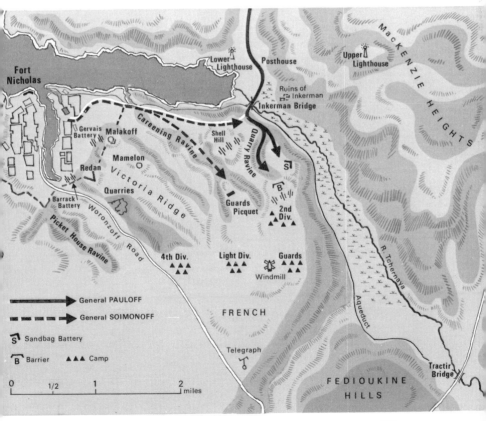

life – another had brought away an artillery saddle, a third a knapsack.

They remained near the bridge for about half an hour unmolested; but when they crossed over and moved back along the causeway, they came under fire again from allied artillery brought forward on the hill. Not all went back over the bridge. The Boutirsk Regiment who had originally been part of Pauloff's field army straggled back towards Sebastopol along a narrow road which proved difficult going for their artillery. It was fortunate for these gunners that Colonel Todleben had ridden out to see how things were shaping, for he was able to restore some sort of order, forming a rearguard out of two battalions of the Boutirsk Regiment and ordering them to stay on guard until every gun had entered the town.

According to Hodasevich, the Russian loss in rank and file approached 12,300, and there were many officer casualties as well, including twenty-eight out of fifty in the Taroutine Regiment. After it was all over, Prince Mentschikoff was entirely at a loss how to send the bad news to the Tsar after a favourable report he had despatched in the morning. Accordingly a council of war was held where it was resolved that General Dannenberg himself should go to St. Petersburg and tell the Emperor what had happened; for as Grand Duke Nicholas said, 'Your Excellency knows well the ground and your own plan of attack, so I should advise you to go yourself and relate to my father all the particulars in order to prevent mistakes.' Still, the long journey to St. Petersburg could not have been very agreeable to the general, giving as it did so much time to reflect that at the end of it he would have to stand before the Emperor and report the defeat of the attack he had planned.

Thus, as confirmed by these complementary reports from both sides, the Battle of Inkerman ended in a victory for the English. By holding the many Russian fierce attacks on their left and centre, by neutralizing the great Russian batteries on Shell Hill, and by hurling out, with the help of the French, the Russians from the Sandbag Battery on the right, they managed to win a decisive battle of the war. It now only remained for the allies to storm Sebastopol; but this was to take many months to accomplish.

FLORENCE NIGHTINGALE

FLORENCE NIGHTINGALE

'The custom of the service did not aim to provide facilities, medical or otherwise, up to the lofty standards of Miss Florence Nightingale.'

At Inkerman Sir George Cathcart was killed, and the battle also saw the end of the Duke of Cambridge's command. He was prostrated by nervous exhaustion from the stress of it, and sought to recuperate aboard the *Restitution*. The great storm found him still there, and he was made more upset by the buffeting. Much to the dismay of Queen Victoria, he then chose to quit the seat of war. She believed that leaving the Crimea before the end of hostilities would make a bad impression – particularly because he was a royal duke as well as a general. She thought it might even ruin his military career. However, he survived; he became a field-marshal in 1862, and later commander-in-chief.

Other casualties at this time were Lord Lucan and Lord Cardigan. Lord Lucan wrote a letter to the Secretary for War complaining of the assessment of his conduct in command of the cavalry at Balaclava in Lord Raglan's despatches. To his surprise, this led to his being asked to resign. On 14 February 1855 he left the Crimea. By then Lord Cardigan had already departed. The severe winter weather proved too much for his health, compelling him to stay on his yacht for four or five days at a time. On 19 November 1854 he asked Lord Raglan for leave of absence on sick certificate. Lord Raglan insisted on a medical board, and this found him unfit for duty. On 12 December 1854 he left for home, where on arrival he was welcomed as a hero.

Meanwhile, Private Wightman of the 17th Lancers had been swept into captivity. The Cossacks who took him prisoner were very rough, hauling their captives along by the tails of their coats and driving lance-butts into their backs to stir them on. When they reached the Tchernaya, the Russians were as kind to them as the Cossacks had been brutal before: for some, water was fetched, to others, vodka was given. They were then conveyed in bullock-carts to a village a little distance in the rear, where their wounds were attended to. Wightman placed on the window-ledge

Officers of the 4th Light Dragoons

the bullet extracted from his knee. The Russian sentry took it and asked by signs if it had wounded Wightman. When he nodded, the Russian spat on it and threw it out of the window exclaiming, 'Sukin sin!' – son of a bitch. A strange thing happened that afternoon. Private John Bevin of the 8th Hussars had been having his wounds dressed, and a Russian cavalryman lying on the opposite of the hut, with two sword-cuts on the head and three fingers off, had been watching him for some time. At last the Russian got up, crossed the floor, and made Bevin understand that he was responsible for his wounds. Bevin cheerfully owned to the charge, and, pointing to a fragment of his own right ear, gave the Russian to understand 'that it was he who had played the part of St Peter'. Whereupon the two fraternized, and Bevin had to resort to much artifice to escape being kissed by the battered Muscovite.

About four the same afternoon, when they were all very stiff and sore, General Liprandi, the Russian commander, paid them a visit. He was very pleasant and spoke excellent English. 'Come now, men,' he asked, 'what did they give you to drink? Did they prime you up with spirits to make you charge us in such a mad way?'

192

William Kirk of the 17th Lancers, an unwounded prisoner who had lost his horse, was leaning against the door when General Liprandi spoke. He had been punishing the Russian vodka a bit, and he stepped up to the General and said, 'You think we were drunk? By God, I tell you that if we had as much as smelt the barrel, we would have taken half Russia by this time!' General Liprandi looked at him with a smile and replied good-humouredly, 'Indeed then to be sure we should have had a poor chance.' Sergeant-Major Fowler of the 4th Light Dragoons had been run through the back by a Cossack lance, and was sitting in the corner. He was a fine dignified soldier, a gentleman born, and one of the handsomest men in the Light Brigade. Raising himself with great pain and difficulty, for his wound had stiffened, he stood upright and severely checked Kirk for his impertinence; then coming smartly to attention before Liprandi, and saluting the general, he said with great earnestness, 'On my honour, sir, except for the vodka your men have given to some of us, there is not a man who has tasted food or drink this day. We left camp before daylight, and were continuously in the field until we became prisoners of war. Our uncooked rations are still in our haversacks. Our daily issue of a mouthful of rum is made in the afternoon, and, believe me, sir, we don't hoard it. I wish all the men who have gone to their account this day were as free of sin as they were of drink!' Liprandi was moved. 'You are noble fellows,' said he, 'and I am sincerely sorry for you. I will order you some vodka, and will send you also some pens, ink and paper, for some of you at least have parents, wives or sweethearts; so write and tell them that they can rely on your being well treated.'

Soon after the general had gone, the surgeons entered and set about amputating a leg of each of four men. They did not use chloroform, but simply sprinkled cold water on the poor fellows' faces. It seemed a butcherly job, and certainly was a sickening sight; nor was any good purpose served, for each of the sufferers died immediately on the removal of the limb. At night they were served out, instead of blankets, with the greatcoats which the Turks had left behind when they evacuated the redoubts. They swarmed with vermin, but the night was bitterly cold, and they were very acceptable. Next morning General Liprandi paid them another visit to tell them that a flag of truce had been sent to him from the English camp, requesting permission to bury the dead; and that he had replied that the Russians were Christians and would undertake the decent interment of the English dead. He then asked whether they had any idea how many horses had been killed. Of course they had not, and he told them 404. As he was leaving, he again denounced the charge as 'sheer madness' but repeated that they were 'noble fellows'.

That same night they started for Simpheropol in one-horse carts, two men in a cart lying on straw. They travelled by night, covering the fifty miles in four marches. At the halting-place at Livadia a Russian officer annexed Wightman's spurs, but was civil enough to give him twenty copecks for them, which coin the Russian orderlies stole when carrying him into Simpheropol Hospital. When they were stripped, most of the uniforms were so stiff with blood that they could have stood on end of themselves. After a week's rest, it was found that the wounded limbs of several poor fellows were mortifying, and amputation in those cases was resorted to, but with very bad results, for of nine men operated on only one survived. On 3 November the Grand Dukes Nicholas and Michael came to Simpheropol on their way to Sebastopol, and paid them a visit in the hospital. They asked them whether they were comfortable, and if they could do anything for them. Laying aside shyness in the presence of so great personages, they bluntly complained of the food served, which consisted of black bread, each loaf weighing from thirty to forty pounds, cabbage soup, which was to them horrible, made as it was of cabbage, small lumps of meat, vinegar and oil, which mixture was boiled in a large iron pot with garlic, after which the pot was brought into the ward, and the order of the day was that they should all sit round it with great wooden spoons and dip into it for luck. He was indeed a fortunate man who chanced to fish out one of the spare morsels of meat. The Grand Duke Nicholas said he was aware that it was not English soldiers' diet, but that it was exactly the same ration on which the Russian soldiers were marching and fighting; and he added that as they got farther into the interior of Russia, they would find the food would improve. He said it was a great pity to see such fine men knocked about as they had been; and before leaving, told them that any complaints that they should desire to make, they were to report the same just as if they were with their own regiments, and they might rely that they would be inquired into. Plenty of visitors came to see them daily. A kind French lady frequently brought them wine, grapes and biscuits; she would go down on her knees by the bedside of the poor fellows who were waiting for death and pray with them. The wounded Russians brought in after the battle of Inkerman died like flies; every morning five or six carts piled high with dead bodies passed their windows on the way to the dead-pit. Every hole and corner of the great hospital was crammed with wounded men, three out of four of whom were the victims of bayonet wounds, so that the fighting must have been very close. They looked anything but pleasantly at the English, and indeed there was one row. William Kirk of the Lancers, lying sick in the next ward among a lot of Russian soldiers, was spat on by two of them. He was up like a shot, and went at the crowd of them with his fists. After a struggle he was overpowered, thrust by the orderlies into something like a strait-jacket, and tied down on his bed, where he remained till the evening, when the surgeons released him, threatening him with severe punishment if he used his fists again. He died very soon after, and there was a suspicion that he had been poisoned.

When they became convalescent they were able to quit hospital and were sent on the march farther into the interior. Each man received an outfit of long boots, a sheepskin coat and a black coat, two rough shirts, pieces of rag for socks, and a fur cap with flaps. It was on Christmas afternoon in 1854 that they were removed from the hospital to the prison. The sergeant of the guard sold for them the Turkish greatcoats they had no further need of, and bought vodka for them from the proceeds. They kept their Christmas sitting round a big fire, passing the bottle until the vodka had all gone, the Russian guards sharing with them as boon companions. Next morning, in a blustering freezing snowstorm, they began their march in company with a gang of convicts in leg-irons and each handcuffed to a long chain. They were soldiers who had misbehaved at Inkerman, most of them Poles, and bound for Siberia. Wightman's knee was still stiff, and he walked with a crutch, and soon fell behind. Two men of the escort were sent back for him, and the good fellows, pitying his painful condition, made a seat with their muskets and in this 'king's chair', with an arm round the neck of each, they carried him to the end of the day's march. During the rest of the long journey, which lasted several days, he travelled by the officer's order in a bullock-cart. The Englishmen and the escort were very friendly together, and they marched along singing and laughing, linked arm and arm. They were billeted at night in the filthy huts of the Russian villages they passed through, and it must have been in the foul air of those stinking hovels where three of them, including Wightman, caught a violent fever, for which they were left behind in the hospital at Alexandrovska, where they were well treated, and received great kindness. Poor Brown died two days after admission, but Harris and Wightman were well enough at the end of the month to resume the march. At Akaterinovslow, a large and fine

Captain Brown, 4th Light Dragoons, and servant in winter dress

city, they were joined by three French soldiers, two of them were prisoners of war, one a deserter; and by two English infantrymen who were deserters. The Russian soldiers hated deserters, and they always got the roughest of treatment. While the prisoners of war were billeted and were regarded by the escort as comrades, the deserters were shoved into the prisons and were seen only on the march. At the daily roll-call before starting, when a prisoner's name was called, he would be patted on the back and called a 'good man': when a deserter answered to his name, he would be pushed rudely to one side, spat on, and called a 'Sukin sin'. The English prisoners would not speak to the fellow countrymen who were deserters; but they felt sorry for one French deserter when he told his story. When in the advanced trenches, he said, his party were much annoyed by the fire of a Russian sharpshooter in an adjacent rifle-pit, and their officer exclaimed that he wished to God someone would kill the fellow. Presently this man, by his own account, crept forward in the darkness, shot the sharpshooter and ran back under heavy fire from both sides. On his return instead of praising him as expected the officer ordered his arrest. In a passion the man ran at the officer, knocked him down, leapt out of the trench, and ran to the Russians under fire.

During the three weeks' march from Ekaterinovslow to Kharkoff they met from time to time large bodies of reinforcements going towards Sebastopol, consisting for the most part of old men and young lads scarcely able to carry their rifles. They would point them at the English prisoners and shout, 'Angleski! Sevastopol!' The prisoners advised them to make haste, because for the present the English had not got many Russians to shoot at! At Kharkoff they were quartered in the prison, but there were few restrictions, and they were kindly treated. In fact, as General Liprandi had said, the farther they got into Russia, the better they were treated; and this was the case in their subsequent moves to Veronesh and finally Odessa. All in all the lot of English prisoners in Russian hands was not a hard one – provided they managed to keep alive.

After the Battle of Inkerman came the winter of discontent. It has been said that the Tsar's best generals were General Janvier and General Février. Certainly these two almost defeated the English in 1855. The muddy road from Balaclava up on to the plateau by the Col to the trenches around Sebastopol was well nigh impassable for much of the winter. Stores, food, medicaments, and, above all, fuel and wood for the fires were in very short supply. A soldier's bed in the trenches was often mud with wet blankets, and more died from semi-starvation and disease than from enemy bullets. Depending on the changeable weather, they were either ankle-deep in mud and wet to the skin, or frozen stiff from head to foot. Smitten with cholera, scurvy, gangrene, fevers, frost-bite and dysentery, the fine army which had fought so gallantly at Alma, Balaclava and Inkerman withered away. Even if the wounded and sick were got back to the base hospitals at Scutari, they usually died there. The Medical Department had broken down like the Commissariat, and until the arrival of Florence Nightingale, the sick had often less chance of recovering in hospital than they had in the trenches. The French, meanwhile, with their shorter lines of communications, and with a government and commissariat possessing more foresight and ability, were in better shape. Before the winter of 1854–5 the British did most of the fighting; afterwards, the French took over the rôle of leader of the allies.

The road past Kadikoi church where Surgeon Munro had his hospital

Although the conditions in the trenches before Sebastopol were terrible during the first winter, it was almost as bad, according to Mrs. Duberly, in and around Balaclava. In her diary she wrote:

'If anyone should ever wish to make a model Balaclava in England, he should take a village of ruined houses and hovels in the extremest state of all imaginable dirt; allow the rain to pour inside and outside them until the whole place was a swamp of filth ankle-deep; catch about, on an average, 1,000 sick Turks with the plague, cram them into the houses indiscriminately; kill about 100 a day, and bury them so as to be scarcely covered with earth, leaving them to rot at leisure – taking care to keep up the supply. On to one part of the beach drive all the exhausted supply ponies, dying bullocks, and worn-out camels, and leave them to die of starvation. They will generally do so in about three days, when they will begin to rot and smell accordingly. Collect together from the water of the harbour all the offal of the animals slaughtered for the use of the occupants of above 100 ships, to say nothing of the inhabitants of the town – which, together with an occasional floating human body, whole or in parts, and the driftwood of the wrecks, pretty well covered the water – and stew them all up together in a narrow harbour, and you will have a tolerable imitation of Balaclava. If that is not *piquante* enough, let some men be instructed to sit and smoke on the powder-barrels landing on the quay. That is what I saw to-day!'

The hardships suffered by the soldiers around Balaclava and in the trenches before Sebastopol brought new habits and innovations. Some having sought solace with hubble-bubble pipes, and not liking them, tried smoking tobacco rolled in paper. This Turkish style of smoking cigarettes became popular and, having spread throughout the army, was copied back at home. Then to meet the vagaries of the Russian climate woollen balaclava helmets to cover the ears were evolved, and to keep the body warm, cardigans and raglan overcoats. In hot weather, hats were worn wrapped with gauze which could be let down to keep off flies and mosquitoes; in cold weather – and the Crimean winters were very cold – well-adapted fur clothing appeared, and some elegant

Balaclava harbour in winter

Balaclava

examples are shown being worn by Captain Brown and his servant.

With the coming of spring, the scene and allied prospects both brightened: vegetation and lovely flowers covered over the sores of battle so that Mrs. Duberly could once more enjoy her rides around the front and through the camps. Indeed, life in the allied camps during the quiet times before the final phases of the war was relatively pleasant. During this period Lady George Paget arrived at Balaclava to be with her husband. She had been staying with Lord and Lady Stratford de Redcliffe at Constantinople and arrived with them in the *Caradoc*. The first few days were spent riding round the camps and viewing from the top of the eastern cliff of the plateau the fields of the Charge of the Light Brigade and the Battle of Inkerman. Near the latter the cavalcade was fired on from the heights opposite, but the shot fell well short. On 20 May Lord George's cousin in the navy, through the good

200

offices of Admiral Lyons, arranged an expedition by steamer along the south coast. The party consisted of, besides his cousin Lord Clarence Paget, General and Mrs. Estcourt, the wife of Admiral Grey, Captain Keppel, Lord Burghersh, Sir Hugh Rose, Colonel Dundas, Sir Thomas Whichcote and Captain Calthorpe; so there were three ladies on board. A feature of the field of Balaclava is the Woronzoff Road running along the Causeway Heights beside the six redoubts manned by the Turks before the battle. This road runs from Sebastopol to the seaside château of Prince Woronzoff at Alupka near Yalta. Prince Woronzoff had been Russian Ambassador in London, and Captain Calthorpe had stayed with him before the war; and he persuaded the ship's captain to take the vessel near inshore so that the party on board could take a good look at the château's beautiful terraced gardens with their statuary and conservatories. As they approached, however, the sound of musket shots was heard, and bullets splashed in the sea around them. On this, they lined the three ladies on the rail while the men pretended to hide behind them 'to put the Ruskies to the blush' as Lord George expressed it. This had the desired effect. Ashamed of what they had done, the Russians stopped firing. The steamer then went on its way so that the party might view the beautiful coast as far as Yalta. On their return, as they passed the château, they were greeted with cheers. (When Prince Woronzoff was in London he had chosen Edward Blore to design this château for him. It was the same house which Churchill and his staff occupied during the Yalta Conference of 1945.)

The rest of Lady George's stay until her return to Constantinople on 7 July 1855 was spent in riding out over the field of Balaclava, going to the Sardinian camp at Kamara, visiting the Sanatorium Hospital on the Balaclava Heights, and, until his premature death, entertaining and being entertained by the commander-in-chief. Lord Raglan used to send his carriage down to the harbour for Lady George to fetch her up to his headquarters for luncheon; after which with a number of staff they rode out through the camps, going as far as the Quarries in front of the Light Division Camp, which was almost in the front line. It was a curious sight to see a lady riding alongside a general to the field of battle; and the soldiers left in the camps would turn out to cheer them. However, they always cheered Lord Raglan. It was not just because of the lady's presence. He was immensely popular with everyone in the army in spite of the privations suffered from exposure and lack of supplies during the terrible previous winter, for which they might justly have considered him largely responsible as their commander. Lord Raglan disliked the men cheering him. He believed that if he allowed them to cheer him on one occasion, they might well turn out to curse him on the next. Also it offended his shy nature to receive applause. According to Lady George, he would try to escape the groups of men on their route ahead. He would lead her off along by-ways to avoid their embarrassing cheers.

On other occasions, the Pagets rode out together to hear the Sardinians' band play outside Kamara church. Lord George could not help contrasting the turn-out of the officers of the Sardinians – and to some extent of the French – with that of British officers. The former, he said, were *'tirés à quatre épingles'*, with everything as neat as if they were strolling through the streets of Genoa or Paris, while it would seem to be a pride among British officers to rival each other in the opposite direction. The younger they were the more slovenly and dirty was their appearance and dress. It was some comfort to him that the cavalry at least made some attempt to look like gentlemen.

The Sardinian army was the admiration of all; perfect in every detail. Their camp equipage of all sorts, their clothing, the appearance of their men on parade, were unexceptionable, while the Bersaglieri with their picturesque hats rivalled the Zouaves. Their camp was also beyond praise: every hut and tent decorated in perfect taste, even down to their theatre; and all sprung up like magic before they had been a week on the ground. The superb band played most afternoons outside Kamara church, a popular rendezvous, and was much in demand by the allies for social and state occasions. It wanted but the Battle of Tchernaya to prove later their prowess on the battlefield. It is true they came out a very small army, spick and span from their own country, and into the midst of men recovering from a Crimean winter, and therefore the contrast was striking; still, according to Lord George, it was greater than it should have been.

Lady George's excursions were not all frivolous. Towards the end of her stay she was making regular visits to the Sanatorium Hospital above Balaclava. She took newspapers and writing material for the wounded. She soon formed a warm friendship with Miss Shaw Stewart and became full of admiration for the way the hospital was run. As Lord George was not allowed into the huts, he spent many a long hour lying on the grass at the edge of the cliffs below the castle waiting for his wife. To start with she only visited a few huts; but when the word got around of the
202

Miss Florence Nightingale.
at Embley
December 28th 1857.

'strange beautiful lady visitor' the others did not like being left out; and she was persuaded to do the complete rounds of the hospital on each visit.

By this time the reform of army nursing by Florence Nightingale and the re-organization of army catering by M. Soyer had begun.

Florence Nightingale arrived at Scutari opposite Constantinople on 3 November 1854. The Barrack Hospital had proved a death trap rather than a sanatorium; and much to the consternation of Dr. John Hall, Chief of Medical Staff to the British Expeditionary Force, had been extremely unfavourably reported on. Florence Nightingale, as is well known, revolutionized the administration of Barrack Hospital and restored its proper functions, dominated its doctors and disciplined its nurses. Six months later when the Barrack Hospital was reasonably satisfactory, she wanted to go to the Crimea. Here were two British

The Sanatorium Hospital at Balaclava

Ward of the Barrack Hospital at Scutari

hospitals, both at Balaclava. One, the General Hospital, had been established near the harbour at the time of the first arrival of the British in September 1854. It was another hospital in Dr. John Hall's charge on which the Sanitary Commission had reported adversely. The enormous numbers of sick, from cholera, from wounds received at Balaclava in October and at Inkerman in November, and from undernourishment and exposure during the following winter had necessitated further accommodation, and a hospital of huts, called the Sanatorium Hospital or Castle Hospital, had been set up on the heights near the old Genoese castle above Balaclava. Both hospitals had a staff of female nurses, and disquieting news had reached Florence Nightingale of the nurses' conduct, particularly at the General Hospital. The matron of the Sanatorium was Lady George's friend Miss Shaw Stewart, the sister of Sir Michael Shaw Stewart, M.P. She had had experience of nursing in Germany and London, and, being a bit of a martinet, was quite capable of controlling her staff; but the other hospital seemed in a bad state. However, a fatal flaw in Miss Nightingale's instructions had appeared, and her authority in the Crimea was questioned. Details of her standing, her instructions and the assistance to be given her had been sent to Lord

Raglan, Lord Stratford de Redcliffe, the British Ambassador, and Dr. John Hall. But Lord Raglan was occupied in storming Sebastopol and Lord Stratford was indifferent. Dr. John Hall therefore seized a chance of getting 'a bit of his own back' for the criticism to which he had been subject because of Florence Nightingale. He asserted that as her instructions named her 'Superintendent of the Female Nursing Establishment in the English Military Hospitals in Turkey', she had no jurisdiction in the Crimea. The nurses had been aware of this. Supported by Dr. Hall and preferring his easy-going ways to the high standards imposed by Florence Nightingale, many had volunteered to go to Balaclava to escape her discipline. For example, Miss Clough had gone to join 'Sir Colin Campbell's Hospital above Balaclava'; inspired, she said, by romantic enthusiasm for the Highland Brigade, but really, as she confided to her friends, 'to escape direct supervision from Miss Nightingale'. Next, Mrs. Elizabeth Davis, a constant rebel at Scutari, volunteered to go to the General Hospital at Balaclava against Florence Nightingale's wishes and was allowed by Dr. Hall to proceed. She assumed command of the kitchen and conducted the catering with rollicking extravagance, rejoicing in feeding up young officers who were her special pets.

It appeared as if Dr. Hall were trying to thwart Florence Nightingale by a legal quibble, and she decided to visit the Crimea all the same. Soon after she arrived there Surgeon Munro of the 93rd Highlanders saw her riding off to inspect the British camps before Sebastopol, and her reputation as the beloved 'Lady of the Lamp' at Scutari having reached the battle front, the soldiers turned out to cheer her wherever she went. However, before she could even attempt to reform the General Hospital, she became a patient there herself. Smitten with 'Crimean Fever', she collapsed, and it was with difficulty that she was nursed back to health and shipped off to Scutari.

It was not only the medical services that were improved after the visit of the Sanitary Commission. Catering was revolutionized through the agency of a distinguished and most unlikely volunteer, comparable in his own sphere to Florence Nightingale. Alexis Soyer, maître chef of the Reform Club, arrived in March 1855 with full authority from Lord Panmure who as War Secretary had succeeded Sidney Herbert, sponsor of Florence Nightingale. This was after the fall of Lord Aberdeen's government mainly due to the collapse of the administrative services in the Crimea.

In manner and appearance Soyer was a comic opera Frenchman,

206

but Florence Nightingale recognized his genius. 'Others,' she wrote, 'have studied cooking for the purpose of gourmandizing, some for the show; but none but he for the purpose of cooking large quantities of food in the most nutritious and economical manner for great numbers of people.' Though those on the spot received him coolly, Soyer was armed with authority, and he proceeded to attack the kitchens of the hospitals. He composed recipes for using army rations to make excellent soup and stews. He put an end to the traditional system of boiling everything. He insisted on having permanently allocated to the kitchens soldiers who could be trained as cooks. He invented special stoves, ovens to bake bread and biscuits, and a Scutari teapot which made and kept tea hot for fifty men. Tactfully, he gave a luncheon attended by Lord Stratford de Redcliffe and his wife at which he served delicious dishes made from army rations. Soyer won everlasting fame for the 'soyer' stove for use in barracks and the field, familiar to all who have served in the army during the last hundred years.

The hospitals were bad, the nursing inadequate and the feeding deplorable until the advent of Florence Nightingale and maître chef Soyer; but to give him his due, Dr. John Hall, the Chief of

Soyer's New Field Stove

Medical Staff, was not altogether to blame – and he certainly put up a spirited defence of himself. The custom of the service did not aim to provide facilities, medical or otherwise, up to the lofty standards of Miss Florence Nightingale. Under more normal conditions than found in the Crimea Dr. Hall's arrangements might well have proved adequate. It was the combination of circumstances which proved too much for his medical administration. To the ravages of cholera and dysentery, for which he was in no way responsible, were added exposure to extreme weather conditions of cold and wet, and a large flow of wounded from the battlefields. To contribute to his troubles, wordy inaccurate journalists sent home emotive despatches laying bare to the receptive public in England all that was wrong; and this had never happened before!

Not all the hospitals were bad even before Florence Nightingale arrived. The Sanatorium Hospital on the Heights above Balaclava was well run by Miss Shaw Stewart, and from the start Surgeon Munro of the 93rd Highlanders set up an admirable hospital for his regiment in the church at Kadikoi. It was the combination of several adverse factors which devastated the British army in the first winter of the war; and neither Lord Raglan nor Dr. John Hall were solely to blame. Cholera was a major factor. Many died of it in Bulgaria, as many as 10,000 Frenchmen; and men were dropping out in considerable numbers, and dying of it, even in the healthy September sunshine on the march towards Sebastopol. It is said to have begun in the French transports soon after leaving Marseilles. Certainly the French suffered most to start with, and there were comparatively few British victims in Bulgaria. However, cholera flourished among the starving ill-clad British soldiers before Sebastopol, and it must be admitted that the French with their shorter lines of communication to Kamiesch, and with a government and commissary possessing more foresight and ability, were in better shape than the British after the first terrible winter.

No one knew the cause of cholera or how to prevent or contain it, but a study of Surgeon Buzzard's experiences is interesting. Surgeon Buzzard joined Omar Pasha's Turkish army at Balaclava after the battle. In his journal he noted that soon after his arrival, Admiral Boxer, who was in charge of the harbour, died of cholera, as had his nephew a few days previously. The Sardinian contingent encamped near him lost 200 men from it in a few days, and the Guards and the 31st also suffered badly. The Turkish troops were not so much affected, but with them there was a large amount of

208

preliminary diarrhoea representing a slight attack. Surgeon Buzzard alone completely escaped, remaining in perfect health. He believed he owed this to the precautions he took based on previous knowledge of the disease. The year before, when he was a doctor in Soho, a sudden and terribly severe outbreak of cholera had occurred, which caused an unprecedented mortality. For three weeks he was actively engaged night and day in the district lending a hand. There he had the good fortune to get to know Dr. Snow, acknowledged later as responsible for the discovery that cholera is conveyed through the medium of drinking water. He was the senior local doctor in Soho, and Buzzard went with him on his rounds, thereby becoming more and more convinced that Dr. Snow was right. As in the case of most great discoveries it was a long time before Dr. Snow's views were accepted, and Buzzard recalled that at first they were ridiculed. However, Surgeon Buzzard came to the Crimea convinced that cholera was most frequently conveyed through infected drinking water, and that the very best way of escaping it was to drink only boiled water, tea, coffee or a very light ale which had been sent out in large quantities by an exporter and was on sale by a sutler at Kadikoi. He tried to make others follow his example; but they were incredulous, and would not do so. As the evidence which Dr. Snow had accumulated was not published before 1855, after the British army had left England, he felt practically certain that he was probably the only person in the Crimea who really knew how to protect himself against cholera.

THE BATTLE OF THE TCHERNAYA AND THE FALL OF SEBASTOPOL

THE BATTLE OF THE TCHERNAYA AND THE FALL OF SEBASTOPOL

'Si ça coûte dix ou dix milles, nous le prenons.'
GENERAL PÉLISSIER

In the spring of 1855, following a successful expedition to Kertch at the east end of the Crimea to cut one of the main Russian supply routes, serious plans were set in being to take Sebastopol. Although the siege had lasted eight months, the allies were still little nearer entering the town; while in the meantime, under the able direction of Colonel Todleben, the Russian defences had been considerably strengthened. On the other hand, General Pélissier, a new French commander of drive and initiative, had been appointed, and the French army was expanded to 90,000 men. Noted for his ruthlessness, Pélissier was ready to attack Sebastopol without regard to cost. The British were now in the centre with the larger French forces on either side of them. The plan was for the French on the left to carry out holding and feint operations while the French on the far right attacked a strong point known as the Mamelon. *'Si ça coûte dix ou dix mille, nous le prenons,'* Pélissier announced dramatically, referring to the impending French assault on the Mamelon. Beyond the hill of the Mamelon was the even stronger fortress, the Malakoff, which all now agreed was the key to Sebastopol; but the Mamelon had to be taken first. A rather similar situation faced the British in the centre. A minor stronghold, the Quarries, had to be taken before the more formidable Redan beyond it could be attacked.

The allied assault began with a bombardment from 550 guns, after which the British trenches in front of the Quarries were filled up with the first storming party of about 400 men, while the French for their part assembled as many as four brigades. After the firing of a number of rockets, the guns ceased firing and the attack began. The French troops rushed across the 500 yards

213

separating them from their objective and were soon swarming up the walls of the Mamelon. After planting the tricolour on the captured fortress, the Zouaves went on without orders to take the Malakoff itself, but were soon driven back. When Lord Raglan saw the Zouaves entering the Mamelon, he gave the signal for his 400 waiting storming troops to charge the Quarries. This they did with such dash that they took the Russians by surprise and drove them back into the Redan. The success of these two operations sent a wave of optimism through the allied camps. 'Johnny Russ is done for,' was a common remark now, and an early end of the war was fully expected.

The next phase was an attack by the French on the keypoint of the Sebastopol defences, the Malakoff; and the British, determined to lend a hand, decided to try to take the Redan. Their pride would not allow them to stand by and watch the French take Sebastopol on their own, even though the fall of the Malakoff would make the capture of the Redan unnecessary. The Redan

General Pélissier

Sergeants of the Royal Artillery with trophies

was a very strong place indeed. Its two faces met at an angle jutting towards the British like a battleship. It had a fortified earthwork at its base and a twenty-foot ditch in front of it. Out in front again was an abatti of tangled sharpened branches of trees eight feet high. Lord Raglan felt confident that the bombardment would break all this down as well as silence the many Russian guns. He could not have been more wrong. In fact everything went awry with both the first attacks. Pélissier had planned to allow two hours of daylight in which the guns could pulverize the repairs to their defences achieved by the Russians during the night before the attack. Then at the last moment, at the request of a new commander, he put forward his attack to first light, and Raglan agreed to advance the British attack as well. This change of plan brought the usual sequence of order, counter-order, disorder; and in the end the French attack started even before the earlier zero hour, as a mortar shell with a trailing light was mistaken for the signal rocket. Then some French divisions insisted on finishing a leisurely meal, and what was meant as a joint attack got off to a very ragged start. The Frenchmen attacking the Gervais Battery alongside the Malakoff fared worst. Not a Frenchman crossed the ditch.

When Lord Raglan saw that the French were failing to take the Malakoff, he decided that although there had been no morning bombardment to soften up its defences he must order his troops to attack the Redan to ease the Russian pressure on his allies. But to make matters worse the Redan was not even shelled while the British were preparing to attack. By some unaccountable blunder the artillery received an order to cease fire. As the men came out of the parallels to cross the 500 yards between the Quarries and the Redan, they were met by direct fire from the Redan, crossfire from the Barrack and Gervais Batteries, and long distance fire from ships in the harbour. There was grape and musketry too. In fact, such a heavy and continuous fire that it was massacre from the start.

Preceded by a covering screen of riflemen, engineers, men carrying wool-bags to fill in the ditch, and soldiers and sailors carrying ladders, there were two storming columns, one to attack each face. Neither of them had the least success. The forward trenches were packed full of oddments from various regiments come up to see the fun. There was no step provided so that the troops could climb easily out of the trenches. The result was that the ladder-men were not followed up closely enough by their storming troops; and when reserves were called for they could not get through. The sailors were stauncher than most. Midshipman Evelyn Wood worked his way right up to the abatti and got such a liking for land fighting that he later transferred into the army. He was awarded the V.C. during the Indian Mutiny and was promoted field marshal after the Boer War. Another who reached the abatti wrote: 'We had some hundred yards to advance across an open plain with guns loaded with grape and canister blazing away at us. My haversack was covered with blood from men shot near me, and so was my sword.' Almost all the officers were soon killed, many while trying in vain by their example to lead forward the men crouching for cover in shell holes. The fire was so heavy that the men could not stand it; and there was nothing to be done but retreat to the trenches.

Only one column under General Eyre on the British left had any success. Nicknamed Eyre's Greyhounds from their custom of being exercised by him at the double, this brigade led by an Irish regiment passed down Picket House Ravine, and, taking the Russians by surprise, threw them out of the cemetery. From there they moved into Sebastopol and occupied some outlying houses. The Irishmen were quick to unearth a store of wine, and many were soon reeling about dressed in women's clothes, dancing around in bonnets and shawls, regardless of the firing. After dark they had to come back, and all their conquests except the cemetery were abandoned.

The British disaster before the Redan brought many changes. Sir George Brown who was in charge of the assault went home, and Lord Raglan, already a sick man, weighed down by his responsibility died ten days after the unsuccessful assault.

The Russians now made one last effort to win the war. They staged another great attack across the Tchernaya on the allied line of communications to Balaclava, this time guarded by the French and Sardinians. The description of this battle is based on the account of *le capitaine* Henri Loizillon and the report of the Sardinian commander General della Mamora. Loizillon was last heard of when from Versailles and Marseilles he was writing to his parents telling them of his eagerness to go to the Crimea. Being in a reserve brigade, he was a late arrival; but now at last he was there. Throughout the war he wrote a series of long, graphic and extremely well-expressed letters to his parents. Now on 21 August 1855, in a letter longer even than usual, he describes the battle which he calls Tractir Bridge, but which is more usually known as the Battle of the Tchernaya.

He wrote that, after the Battle of Inkerman on 5 November 1854, the English army was reduced to half its original size and the assault on Sebastopol had to be postponed. Instead, a long line of *contravallation* was built along the edge of the Chersonese plateau. The position was entrenched and artillery installed so that it was strong enough to resist any Russian attack.

They passed the winter behind this line of *contravallation*; but from eleven o'clock to four each day every French unit sent detachments down into the Balaclava valleys to fetch timber and brushwood – and the Russians always conveniently pulled back to a safe distance and left them unmolested to carry out this task, moving forward again when they withdrew to the plateau again. In the spring, when new French divisions arrived, some were used to reinforce the positions along the cliffs of the plateau, and others to push the Russian line back from the edge of the Cherso-nese plateau. For this purpose, two divisions and all the cavalry and artillery of the reserve under General Canrobert were moved down into North Valley of Balaclava. The cavalry passed over Tractir Bridge and occupied the heights on the far side of the Tchernaya, and the infantry took up positions on the slopes on the near side of the river. At the sight of the French army approaching, the Russians in the area fled in some disorder: they fired a few shots, and then moved off hurriedly leaving behind a number of their baggage wagons.

About midday, most of the French cavalry were withdrawn across the river; and they camped alongside their infantry and artillery, leaving only a small bridgehead across the river at Tractir Bridge. Meanwhile, to strengthen their defences, they refilled, with water from the river, the canal which took drinking water to Sebastopol, and which had previously been emptied to deny the water to the besieged. Next, on the allied right, the Sardinians occupied Tchorgoun and Hasfort Hill south of the river. These new advanced positions offered several advantages: they kept Russian pressure on the allied flank at a distance, and they opened up the valuable extensive grasslands of the Tchernaya valley. For example, in the Baidar region alone there was sufficient forage to supply 20,000 horses for forty days.

Soon, reports from spies told them that the Russians were preparing an attack. Then, at dawn on 16 August 1855, the French outposts saw a huge Russian army approaching from the Mackenzie Heights and the hills stretching towards the Chouliou river which joins the Tchernaya at Tchorgoun. On the allied right, making use of the darkness, and then the mist of early morning, the Russians approached the Sardinians almost unobserved; and on the left the swarm of tirailleurs which preceded the Russian columns were soon over the river, which was fordable in many places, and attacking the French positions. All along the line they hurled themselves against the defenders of the canal. On the extreme left General Camon's whole division moved up to oppose them, and attacking with bayonets fixed drove them back; but this Russian thrust proved to be only a diversion. The main assault was at the bridge where 200 men under General Failly from General Herbillon's division opposed 6,000 Russians. Outnumbered and under heavy artillery fire, General Failly could not hold his ground against the massed Russian attacks so he retired to the hills behind and staged several counter-attacks with the bayonet, offering a stout resistance which in Loizillon's words made him *'le héros de la journée'*. Then came a new swarm of tirailleurs followed by another Russian mass-attack; and General Failly had to retire still farther, and repeat his counter-attacks.

Now help came from several directions at once: General Herbillon sent in his reserves; General Camon, realizing the Russian attack on his front was not the main one, despatched to Failly's aid two regiments under de Wimpffen – promoted briga-

218

dier after Inkerman; and the Sardinians, although hard-pressed themselves, first turned their guns on the flank of the Russian column attacking General Herbillon, and then sent in some of their infantry. The part played by the Sardinians is well described in General della Marmora's own report:

> The Russians under cover of artillery-fire attacked the hill on the extreme right of General Herbillon's division. The first column had crossed the Tchernaya and surmounted the steep ascent of the hill in spite of the fire of the French tirailleurs, when it was vigorously attacked by the French troops in support and hurled back. But a second Russian attack was seen to be mounting, and as I considered from the disposition of the enemy's forces that they only intended to make a demonstration of artillery before our position, while they concentrated

Battle of the Tchernaya

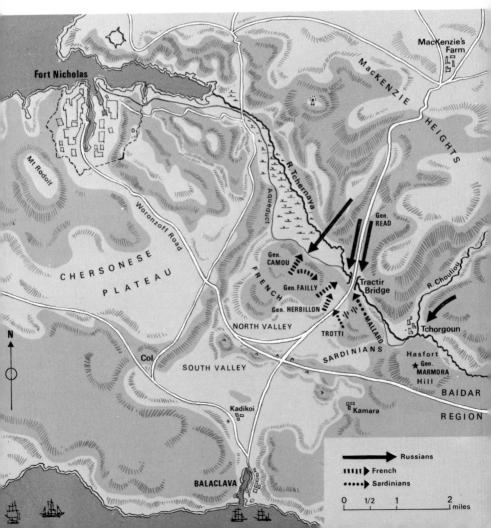

220

Balaclava Harbour

221

The Battle of the Tchernaya or Tractir Bridge

their infantry chiefly on the right of the French on which point a second column was now advancing, I ordered a portion of my fifth brigade under General Mallard to march to the support of the right wing of the French, and I posted two of our batteries in a position from whence they could bring an oblique fire on the Russians. At the same time, I asked the English cavalry under General Scarlett to move down with the Sardinian cavalry into the plain to be in readiness to charge. When the soldiers of the fifth brigade reached the hill, they found that the enemy's attack had been held; but the fire of two batteries from General Trotti's division appeared to do great execution on this second Russian column, which, checked in front by the French troops and harassed in the flank by the fire of our batteries and the musketry of our battalions, fell back in the greatest disorder. I then ordered some of our battalions to advance under cover of rifle-fire from the Bersaglieri; but before this could be carried out the enemy began to retreat, some up the valley of the Chouliou, and the remainder up the road leading to Mackenzie's farm.

Thus the battle of Tractir Bridge ended in another victory for the allies in which, as *le capitaine* Loizillon says, '*les Piémontais* [Sardinians] *ont montré ce dont ils étaient capables et cette journée où ils ont gagné leurs éperons a encore augmenté la confiance que nous avions dans leur armée si coquette.*'

Loizillon was also very proud of what the French had accomplished, saying how splendid it had been for a handful of 4,000 Frenchmen to hold in check 30,000 Russians. This magnificent victory, he says, was gained for a relatively small loss. The French artillery suffered most: one battery of the Guard had forty horses killed and thirty-nine wounded, and three of its officers were wounded. On the other hand, contrary to what was usual, few officers were killed and only about 200 men; and the Russians, he says, had, without exaggeration, 10,000 put out of action. The French took 600 prisoners, and the Sardinians 250; and the allies had also about 1,800 Russian wounded in their ambulances. The Russian prisoners were most unhappy because at the beginning of the war they had been told, quite wrongly, that the French first cut off prisoners' ears and then handed them over to the Turks.

All the ground between the river and the canal was covered with corpses, as was the area around the bridge; while in the river itself bodies were piled one on top of the other. On 18 August there was an armistice to bury the dead, among whom were three Russian generals including General Read who commanded the main Russian attack. On his body was found a letter giving the order for the attack, which had been sent all the way from St. Petersburg and showed that the Tsar had also sent his brother Grand Duke Michael to give assistance.

After the battle of Tractir it became obvious that the Russians were beginning to evacuate Sebastopol and that only patience was required to bring the war to a close. Such a tame ending did not suit the ambitious Emperor Napoleon III and he ordered a final all-out offensive. Pélissier's plan for this consisted of an attack against the southern part of the city at a number of points on a front of over six miles. The French had learnt from the mistakes of the earlier assault and went about their preparations with great thoroughness. Hearing from a spy that the garrison was relieved at midday in the Malakoff, and just at that time the old relief would have marched out and the new relief would not have got in, they chose this moment to attack. Realizing that one of the causes of the first failure was the long distance between their trenches and their objective, they sapped up to within twenty-five yards of the fortress. Finally, to expedite the bringing up of reserves quickly, they built a wide camouflaged road right through their trench system leading directly to the Malakoff. Unfortunately General Simpson who had replaced Lord Raglan was not so efficient. He staged a similar attack to the last one, with even more tragic results.

Zero hour, properly observed this time with synchronized watches, saw the Zouaves bounding across their intervening twenty-five yards like a lot of cats; and without a shot being fired, they were into the Malakoff. Next a bridge of rollers was run across the ditch, and before the Russians had recovered their wits, the fortress was full of French and the tricolour was floating from the ramparts. The tricolour was the alert for the British attack on the Redan, and General Simpson gave the signal for it

Raglan and Pélissier (centre) at Headquarters

by firing four rockets. As on the last occasion, the Russians were ready, and the fire and cross-fire over the 500 yards of open country just as deadly. In spite of severe casualties, however, this time the attackers reached the ditch round the Redan. Here, and in shell holes, the young boys who again made up the bulk of the stormers felt a little safer, but nothing would induce them to go farther. It was the same as on the first attack. The officers got killed trying by their example to lead the men forward. Three officers of the 41st, after vainly striving to induce the men to advance, charged forward together and were all three shot down like one man by the crossfire of the Russians. Finally a general panic seized most of the men, and they rushed suddenly out of the ditch in an effort to get back to the trenches from which they started. In doing so, many of them were shot down like rabbits by the jeering Russians, while others badly wounded crawled or staggered back to safety.

When the cost was counted, it was found that the casualties in two hours nearly equalled those of the whole of the Battle of Inkerman. There were 385 killed, 1,886 wounded, 176 missing, in all 2,447, of whom 156 were officers. General Simpson, as commander-in-chief, came in for most of the blame, and undoubtedly it was a sadly bungled affair, made all the more galling because of the success of the French. To try to put matters right, Sir Colin Campbell was ordered to make an attempt on the following morning with fresh troops from the Highland Brigade and the 3rd Division, who, it is considered, together with the reconstituted Guards Brigade, should have been employed instead of raw youths in the other attack. In the early hours of the morning, however, it was discovered that the Russians had decamped. The seizure of the Malakoff following the defeat of the Russian field army in the battle of the Tchernaya had won the war for the allies. After a few months of manoeuvring and parleying hostilities ended; then on 30 March 1856 peace was declared, and the strange war fought in the Crimea was over.

From the twenty or so eye-witness accounts used in this book the characteristics of the armies of the Crimean War can be discerned, and although on the whole the accounts confirm traditional views, it is worthy of note that they are more sympathetic towards the British commanders than the official histories and show the Russian army as a more attractive organization than usual.

The Turks proved amiable allies, and ingratiating with their 'Ah, Johnny, buono Johnny, buono, buono'; but although for a

225

brief period after their successful defence of Silistria, they were considered staunch, after their flight from the outer Balaclava redoubts Lord Raglan would not allow them to be employed again in the front line.

The Sardinians provided too small a contingent and arrived too late to make much impact; but their contribution to the battle of Tractir won them renown, and they were also respected for the excellence of their equipment: Lord George Paget could not help contrasting their turn-out with the British, his only comfort being that 'the British cavalry officers at least made some attempt to look like gentlemen.'

The French were more professional than the British. At Varna they were embarked long before their allies; at Eupatoria their tricolour was planted on the beach an hour before the first British landed. Before Sebastopol, with their shorter lines of communication and with a more able government and commissariat, they were in better shape, and at the end of the war they showed a great deal more drive and initiative. General Pélissier announced that he would take the Mamelon, a key-point, *'si ça coûte dix ou dix milles'*, and his final storming of the Malakoff was a model of efficiency compared with General Simpson's bungled attempt to storm the Redan. A few advantages, however, lay with the British. The French were not so well disciplined. The French officers could not stop their troops plundering. 'The spirit of the army was so revolutionary that they had little control over their men; they were much surprised at the discipline of the British army.'

The best feature of the British army in the Crimea is usually considered to have been the staunchness of the individual soldier epitomized in the 'Soldier's Battle' at Inkerman. This view is not entirely confirmed. The British soldier was often very brave as is illustrated by Private Wightman's description of the Charge of the Light Brigade; but at times he was no hero. What emerges is not individual bravery by the soldiers, but rather many examples of superb leadership shown by their officers. Sir Colin Campbell is the supreme example. From the start he had his Highlanders well in hand so that they would do anything for him. He made them proud by getting permission to wear their bonnet (shades of Monty, here), he checked them and exhorted them. He said that no soldier should skulk back to the rear on the plea of helping wounded and any who did would be disgraced and their names stuck up in the kirk at home for all to see. Then having warned them, he would turn and encourage them saying: 'Now men the army is watching us. Make me proud of the Highland

226

Brigade!' And he was just as effective with officers. To Lieutenant Roberts on the Marine Heights he exclaimed: 'Go and superintend the formation of a three-gun battery for the sake of an old fellow who has a great deal of responsibility on his shoulders.' Who could fail to do his best when so approached?

Finally the Russians; and surprisingly a picture emerges which is quite different from usual, one which, if Captain Hodasevich alone had to be relied on, might appear suspect, but is confirmed by Private Wightman's records in captivity. To begin with, the Russian army appears far happier than is normally depicted, with

General Simpson

its units possessing strong regimental spirit and love and respect between officer and man. Captain Ermalaev gathers his men around him and asks them if they are going to beat the enemy, and they assure him that they will; and they are all like brothers and friends – just one happy family! This respect felt by the Russians for their aristocratic officers is illustrated on more than one occasion. At Inkerman, Captain Hodasevich drew the attention of his men to Prince Mentschikoff and the Grand Dukes watching their advance. 'Look!' he called. 'Mind you don't disgrace yourself while they are watching you.' Every head turned, and in answer to a further call of Hodasevich of 'Do you see them?' came the reply, 'We do, sir, we do!' Also illustrated is the humane way in which Russians treated their prisoners. General Liprandi is recorded as saying to the cavalrymen in his hands: 'You are noble fellows, and I am sorry for you. I will order you some vodka and will send you also some pens, ink and paper for some of you at least have parents, wives and sweethearts; so write and tell them that they can rely on your being well treated.' All in all, the Russians appear to have been worthy opponents: good fighters, but not too good, and conducting operations in accordance with the recognized courtesies of war in what was one of 'the last of the Gentlemen's Wars'.

BIBLIOGRAPHY

Adye, J.	Recollections of a Military Life (London 1895)
Army lists 1854 and 1969	Hart and H.M.S.O.
Blunt, J.	Letters (National Army Museum)
Burgoyne, R. H.	Records of the 93rd Sutherland Highlanders (London 1883)
Buzzard, T.	With the Turkish Army (London 1915)
Cambridge Modern History	Vol. XI (Cambridge 1909)
Carter, T.	Medals of the British Army – Crimea (London 1861)
Cavendish, A. E. J.	The 93rd Sutherland Highlanders (privately 1928)
Clifford, Henry	Letters and Sketches (London 1956)
Dixon	Crimean War Reminiscences (*R.A. Journal,* Woolwich 1956)
Duberly, Mrs. Henry	Journal (London 1856)
Duberly, Mrs. Henry	Letters to Selina
Ewart, J. A.	A Soldier's Life, Vol. 1 (London 1881)
Fay, Le Général	Souvenirs de la Guerre de Crimée (Paris 1889)
Forrest, Major W.	Letters (National Army Museum)

Gibbs, P.	The Battle of Alma (London 1963)
Greig, Private G.	Diary (Stirling Castle)
Hamley, E.	The War in the Crimea (London 1910)
Hibbert, C.	The Destruction of Lord Raglan (London 1961)
Hitchcock, F. C.	Nolan and Balaclava (*Cavalry Journal* London 1941)
Hitchcock, F. C.	The Light Brigade and Balaclava (*Army Quarterly* 1949)
Hodasevich, R.	Within the Walls of Sebastopol (London 1856)
Jocelyn, J. R. J.	History of Royal Artillery (Crimea Period) (London 1911)
Jones, M.	Charge of the Light Brigade (*R.A. Journal,* Woolwich, 1954)
Kinglake, A. W.	The invasion of the Crimea, 8 Vols. (London 1868)
Loizillon, Henri	Campagne de Crimée – Letters (Paris 1867)
Munro, W.	Records of Service and Campaigning (London 1887)
Nolan, E. H.	History of the War against Russia, 8 Vols. (London 1855–7)
Paget, G.	Light Cavalry Brigade in the Crimea (London 1881)
Peard, G. S.	Campaign in the Crimea (London 1855)
Roberts, H. B. (Lieut. R.M.A.)	Letters (National Army Museum)

Robinson, R.	Diary of the Crimean War (London 1856)
Russell, W. H.	Despatches from the Crimea (London 1966)
Russell, W. H.	The Great War with Russia (London 1895)
Russell, W. H.	British Expedition to the Crimea (London 1877)
Shadwell	Colin Campbell
Todleben, F. E. I.	Défense de Sébastopol, 2 Vols. (St. Petersburg 1863–70)
Whinyates, F. T.	Balaklava (*R.A. Journal* 1895)
Wightman, J. W.	Balaclava Charge (The Nineteenth Century 1892)
Wimpffen, Général de	Crimée – Italie; Notes et Correspondance (Paris 1892)
Woodham-Smith, C.	Florence Nightingale (London 1950)
Woodham-Smith, C.	The Reason Why (London 1953)

APPENDIX A

VICTORIA CROSSES OF THE CRIMEA[1]

*'What is a ribbon worth to a soldier? Everything!
Glory is priceless!'*

SIR E. B. LYTTON, BART.

In 1856 Queen Victoria established a medal to which all ranks of the Army and Navy might aspire. The medal was to be awarded for exceptional bravery, and the Queen named the medal after herself to be known as the Victoria Cross. It took the form of a Maltese Cross cast in bronze attached by a metal 'V' to a bar on which a sprig of laurel is embossed. The Royal Crown with a Lion on top is in the centre of the Cross and beneath the Crown is a scroll inscribed 'For Valour'. The reverse is plain, except that the name and corps of the recipient is engraved on the bar to which the ribbon is attached, and the date of the award is placed in the centre of the Cross.

The names of those awarded the V.C. in the Crimean War are given below. Those mentioned by name in the text have their citation given and are marked by an asterisk. The details of the citation are also given for a few of the others.

Cavalry	in the Charge of the Heavy Brigade or the Charge of the Light Brigade at Balaclava on 25 October 1854:
Second Dragoons	Sergeant-Major John Grieve; Sergeant Henry Ramage.
Fourth Light Dragoons	Private Samuel Parkes* won his award in the Charge of the Light Brigade. Trumpet-Major Crawford's horse was shot and he lost his sword in the fall and

---

1. *From 'Medals of the British Army' by Thomas Carter; dedicated by permission to Major-General the Hon. Sir James Yorke Scarlett, K.C.B. (1868 London).*

233

was attacked by two Cossacks. Parkes placed himself on foot between the Cossacks and Crawford and drove them off with his sword. See p. 156.

Sixth Dragoons

Surgeon James Mouat,* C.B.; Surgeon Mouat, with Sergeant-Major Wooden of the 17th Lancers mentioned below, went to the help of Lieut-Col. Morris, commanding the 17th Lancers, who was lying dangerously wounded in an exposed position after the retreat of the Light Brigade after the Charge (Captain Ewart first discovered him, see p. 168). He dressed Colonel Morris's wounds in the presence of and under heavy fire from the enemy, stopping a serious haemorrhage and helping to save his life.

Eleventh Hussars

Lieutenant Alexander Robert Dunn

Thirteenth Light Dragoons

Sergeant Joseph Malone

Seventeenth Lancers

Sergeant-Major Charles Wooden; Quartermaster-Sergeant John Farrall; Troop Sergeant-Major John Berryman; Berryman also received a clasp at Inkerman.

Royal Artillery

Sergeant-Major Andrew Henry*; for defending the guns of G Battery at the Battle of Inkerman against over-whelming numbers of the enemy and continuing to do so until he received twelve bayonet wounds – see p. 180; Captain and Brevet-Lieutenant-Colonel Collingwood Dickson, C.B.; Brevet-Lieutenant-Colonel Matthew Charles Dixon; Captain Frederick Miller; Captain Gronow Davis; Lieutenant Christopher Charles

Teesdale, C.B.; Sergeant Daniel
Cambridge; Sergeant George Symons;
Gunner and Driver Thomas Arthur.

Royal Engineers   Captain and Brevet-Major Howard
Crauford Elphinstone: on the night of
18 June 1855, after the unsuccessful
attack on the Redan, Elphinstone led a
party of volunteers to retrieve the
scaling ladders left behind after the
assault and eventual repulse. Whilst
doing this he made an extensive search
for the wounded near the enemy lines
and brought back twenty men;
Lieutenant Gerald Graham;
Lieutenant W. O. Lennox; Sergeant
Henry McDonald; Colour-Sergeant
Peter Leitch; Corporal John Moss;
Corporal William Lendrim; Sapper
John Perie.

Grenadier Guards   Private Anthony Palmer: charged with
Brevet-Major Sir Charles Russell into
the Sandbag Battery; defended the
Colours; is said to have saved Sir
Charles Russell's life. Captain and
Lieutenant-Colonel the Hon. H. Hugh
Manvers Percy; Brevet-Major Sir
Charles Russell, Bart.; Sergeant
Alfred Ablett.

Coldstream Guards   Private George Strong who threw a live
shell from a trench before Sebastopol.
Several V.C.'s were awarded for
similar actions as were G.C.'s on the
Russian side, see p. 100; Brevet-Major
Gerald Littlehales Goodlake; Private
William Stanlock.

Scots Fusilier Guards   Brevet-Major Robert James Lindsay,
who stood firm by the Colours when
the Regiment was in confusion; then
led some others into a counter-attack

which repulsed the Russians.
Sergeant Simpson Knox; Sergeant
McKechnie; Sergeant James Craig;
Private William Reynolds.

Infantry of the Line
1st Regt. of Foot

Private Joseph Prosser: on two
occasions, firstly at Sebastopol where
he apprehended a deserter in the face of
enemy cross-fire, then again in front of
Sebastopol where he rescued a
wounded soldier of the 9th in front of
stiff enemy fire.

3rd Regt.

Brevet-Lieutenant-Colonel
Frederick Maude, C.B.; Private John
Connors.

4th Regt.

Private Thomas Grady.

7th Fusiliers

Lieutenant Henry Mitchell Jones,
who on 7 June 1855 led repeated attacks
on the Quarries in front of Sebastopol,
see p. 214, and despite being
wounded stayed at his post till day-
break; Lieutenant William Hope;
Assistant Surgeon Thomas E. Hale,
M.D.; Private William Norman;
Private Matthew Hughes.

17th Regt.

Corporal (Lance-Sergeant) Philip
Smith.

18th Regt.

Captain Thomas Esmonde, at the
Redan, see p. 225, for rescuing
wounded and two days afterwards
extinguishing a live shell.

19th Regt.

Private Samuel Evans; Private John
Lyons.

23rd Regt.

Brevet-Lieutenant-Colonel Edward
W. D. Bell; Sergeant O'Connor;

236

	Assistant Surgeon Henry Thomas Sylvester, M.D.; Corporal Robert Shields.
30th Regt.	Lieutenant Mark Walker.
34th Regt.	Private William Coffey; Private John T. Sims.
41st Regt.	Sergeant-Major Ambrose Madden; Brevet-Major Hugh Mowlands.
44th Regt.	Sergeant William McWheeney.
47th Regt.	Private McDermond.
49th Regt.	Lieutenant John Augustus Conolly; Corporal James Owens; Sergeant George Walters.
55th Regt.	Private Thomas Beach; Brevet-Major Frederick C. Elton.
57th Regt.	Colour-Sergeant George Gardiner; Private Charles McCorrie, for throwing over the parapet a live shell.
68th Regt.	Captain T. de Courcy Hamilton; Private John Byrne.
77th Regt.	Sergeant John Park; Private Alexander Wright.
90th Regt.	Sergeant Andrew Moynihan: at the Redan on 8 September 1855, where he personally killed five Russians and rescued a wounded officer; Private John Alexander.
97th Regt.	Sergeant John Coleman; Brevet-Major Charles Henry Lumley; for having distinguished himself highly by his bravery at the assault on the Redan being among the first inside the work.

The Rifle Brigade	Brevet-Major the Hon. Henry Clifford, for bravery at Inkerman where he led a charge and in it killed a Russian thus saving the life of one of his men; Lieutenant Claude Thomas Bourchier; First Lieutenant William James Cuninghame; Private F. Wheatley; Private R. McGregor; Private Robert Humpston; Private Joseph Bradshaw.
Royal Marines	Lieutenant George Dare Dowell; Corporal John Prettyjohn, for gallantry at Inkerman; Bombardier Thomas Wilkinson for placing sand-bags to repair the work under a galling fire.

Looking at the dates of the above awards it becomes apparent that all these Victoria Crosses were won before the institution of the medal. Thus the Queen struck the medal so as to reward the exceptional deeds carried out by her armed forces during the Crimean campaign. Up till the Crimean War the British soldier could win no medal for acts of bravery, and it was only owing to generosity on the part of officers that soldiers got any reward at all. All the medals above were given after the war, and this made it possible for the award to be given for a series of brave acts – as for example in the case of Private Prosser and of Captain Esmonde – instead of just one as is the practice today.

RUSSIAN CROSS OF ST. GEORGE

The institution of the Victoria Cross was paralleled in Russia by that of the Cross of St. George. The Order of St. George had been founded in 1769 by Catherine the Great for outstanding acts of bravery and courage; but it was only available for high-ranking officers; so in 1807 Alexander I added a Cross of St. George for N.C.O.s and soldiers. This had the figure of St. George on its round central medallion and on the reverse the linked cypher SG (Sanctus Georgius).

Leo Nikolayevich Tolstoy, (1828–1910), the author of *War and Peace* and *Anna Karenina* and moral thinker and reformer, who fought as an ensign in Sebastopol, had earlier nearly won the Cross of St. George. As a junker (officer-cadet) he attacked so bravely the Chechenian positions on the banks of the Michin River in February 1852 in the Caucasus campaign that his superiors wanted to recommend him for the honour, but were unable to do so as he was not yet officially in the army, having no release certificate from his previous civil service job. 'I frankly confess that this little cross is the only one of all the military honours I was vain enough to desire, and this incident has infuriated me beyond words,' he wrote. To make matters worse, in March 1853, he was recommended again, yet failed once more to receive it, because he was at the time under arrest for having played chess with an officer and forgotten his turn on guard duty.

APPENDIX B

The New Titles of the Regiments Mentioned in this Book compared with those in Hart's Army List of 1854.

1854	1969
4th (Royal Irish) Regiment of Dragoon Guards	4th/7th Royal Dragoon Guards
5th (The Princess Charlotte of Wales's) Regiment of Dragoon Guards	5th Inniskilling Dragoon Guards
1st (Royal) Regiment of Dragoons	The Blues and Royals (The Royal Horse Guards and 1st Dragoons)
2nd (Royal North British) Regiment of Dragoons	The Royal Scots Greys (2nd Dragoons)

N.B. due to be amalgamated with the 3rd Carabiniers

1854	1969
4th (The Queen's Own) Regiment of Light Dragoons	The Queen's Royal Irish Hussars
6th (Inniskilling) Regiment of Dragoons	5th Royal Inniskilling Dragoon Guards
8th (The King's Royal Irish) Regiment of Light Dragoons (Hussars)	The Queen's Royal Irish Hussars
11th (or Prince Albert's Own) Regiment of Hussars	The Royal Hussars (10th Royal Hussars and 11th Hussars, Prince Albert's Own)
13th Regiment of Light Dragoons	The 13th/18th Royal Hussars (Queen Mary's Own)
15th (The King's) Regiment of Light Dragoons (Hussars)	15th/19th The King's Royal Hussars
17th Regiment of Light Dragoons (Lancers)	17th/21st Lancers

1st (or Grenadier) Regiment of Foot Guards	Grenadier Guards
Coldstream Regiment of Foot Guards	Coldstream Guards
Scots Fusilier Guards	Scots Guards
1st (The Royal) Regiment of Foot	Scottish Division, The Royal Scots (The Royal Regiment) (1)
3rd (E. Kent) Regiment of Foot (or The Buffs)	The Queen's Division, The The Queen's Regiment (2, 3, 35, 50, 57, 70, 77, 81, 97, 107)
4th (The King's Own) Regiment of Foot	The King's Division, The King's Own Royal Border Regiment (4, 34 and 55)
7th Regiment of Foot (Royal Fusiliers)	The Queen's Division, The Royal Regiment of Fusiliers (5, 6, 7 and 10)
9th (The East Norfolk) Regiment of Foot	The Queen's Division, The Royal Anglian Regiment (9, 10, 12, 16, 17, 44, 48, 56 and 58)
17th (The Leicestershire) Regiment of Foot	The Queen's Division, The Royal Anglian Regiment (9, 10, 12, 16, 17, 44, 48, 56 and 58)
18th (Royal Irish) Regiment of Foot	Disbanded 1922
19th (The 1st Yorkshire North Riding) Regiment of Foot	The King's Division, The Green Howards (Alexandra, Princess of Wales's Own Yorkshire Regiment) (19)
21st Regiment of Foot (Royal North British Fusiliers)	Scottish Division, The Royal Highland Fusiliers (Princess Margaret's Own Glasgow and Ayrshire Regiment) (21, 71, 74)

23rd (The Royal Welsh Fusiliers) Regiment of Foot	The Prince of Wales's Division, The Royal Welsh Fusiliers (23)
30th (The Cambridgeshire) Regiment of Foot	The King's Division, The Lancashire Regiment (Prince of Wales's Volunteers) (30, 40, 59 and 82)
34th (The Cumberland) Regiment of Foot	The King's Division, The King's Own Royal Border Regiment (4, 34 and 55)
41st (The Welsh) Regiment of Foot	The Prince of Wales's Division, The Welch Regiment (41 and 69)
42nd (The Royal Highland) Regiment of Foot	Scottish Division, The Black Watch (The Royal Highland Regiment) (42 and 73)
44th (The East Essex) Regiment of Foot	The Queen's Division, The Royal Anglian Regiment (9, 10, 12, 16, 17, 44, 48, 56 and 58)
47th (The Lancashire) Regiment of Foot	The King's Division, The Royal Regiment (North Lancashire) (47 and 81)
49th (The Princess Charlotte of Wales's, or The Hertfordshire) Regiment of Foot	The Prince of Wales's Division, The Duke of Edinburgh's Royal Regiment (Berkshire and Wiltshire) (49, 62, 66 and 99)
55th (The Westmorland) Regiment of Foot	The King's Division, The King's Own Royal Border Regiment (4, 34 and 55)
57th (The West Middlesex) Regiment of Foot	The Queen's Division, The Queen's Regiment (2, 3, 35, 50, 57, 70, 77, 81, 97 and 107)
63rd (The West Suffolk) Regiment of Foot	The King's Division, The King's Regiment (8, 63 and 96)

243

68th (The Durham) Regiment of Foot (Light Infantry)	The Light Division, The Light Infantry (13, 32, 46, 51, 53, 68, 85, 105 and 106)
71st Highland Regiment of Foot (Light Infantry)	Scottish Division, The Royal Highland Fusiliers (Princess Margaret's Own Glasgow and Ayrshire Regiment) (21, 71 and 74)
77th (The East Middlesex) Regiment of Foot	The Queen's Division, The Queen's Regiment (2, 3, 35, 50, 57, 70, 77, 81, 97 and 107)
79th Regiment of Foot (Cameron Highlanders)	Scottish Division, Queen's Own Highlanders (Seaforth and Camerons) (72, 78 and 79)
88th Regiment of Foot (Connaught Rangers)	Disbanded 1922
90th Regiment of Foot (Perthshire Volunteers) (Light Infantry)	Scottish Division, The Cameronians (Scottish Rifles) (26 and 90) Disbanded 1968
93rd (Sutherland Highlanders) Regiment of Foot	Scottish Division, The Argyll and Sutherland Highlanders (Princess Louise's) (91 and 93), due to be disbanded in 1970
97th (The Earl of Ulster's) Regiment of Foot	The Queen's Division, The Queen's Regiment (2, 3, 35, 50, 57, 70, 77, 81, 97 and 107)
Rifle Brigade	The Light Division, The Royal Green Jackets

LIST OF ILLUSTRATIONS

COLOUR PLATES

BLACK AND WHITE PLATES

CHAPTER HEADS

Introduction: Balaclava Harbour
En Route: The Dardanelles
Bulgaria: Varna
Alma: The Capture of Telegraph Hill
The Flank March: The Heights of Bulganak
The First Bombardment: The entrance to Sebastopol Harbour
The Thin Red Line: Badge of the 93rd Highlanders
The Charge of the Heavy Brigade: The Charge
The Charge of the Light Brigade: The Battle of Balaclava
The 4th Division at Balaclava: The town and harbour of Balaclava
Inkerman: Trumpeters of the Royal Artillery with Eagle
Florence Nightingale: The Hospital at Scutari
The Battle of the Tchernaya and the Fall of Sebastopol:
    The French assault Sebastopol

MAPS
(by Patrick Leeson)

INDEX

249

250

252